Winner In The
MIRROR

Activating Your Superpowers:
Mind, Body, and Spirit

Winner In The
MIRROR

Activating Your Superpowers:
Mind, Body, and Spirit

King Kevin Dorival

Courage To Believe Int'l.

Published by Courage To Believe International, LLC.

"Winner in the Mirror - Activating Your Superpowers: Mind, Body, and Spirit
"Copyright © 2020 by King Kevin Dorival.

Editors: Make Your Mark Publishing Solutions and Evah Dixon
Book Designer:

ISBN: 978-0-9855648-4-1 (paperback)
LCCN: 2020920010

For information on special discounts for bulk purchases, and bookings please contact:
King Kevin Dorival at info@kevindorival.com.
Or visit his website at www.kevindorival.com

Courage to Believe International, LLC.
Mailing Address:
Attn: King Kevin Dorival
P.O. Box, 150071 Atlanta, GA. 30315

1. Self-help/Self-improvement > Spirituality > Mind & Body > Nonfiction.

CONTENTS

Special Note To A Dear Friend,

I'd like to take the time to acknowledge a good friend and great entrepreneur, Daniel Junior "45th" Lubin, who had a special gift of inspiring everyone that he came across. Daniel's favorite word was 'Progress' with a smile. His career had just taken off right before he passed away at the young age of 24 on the 20th of October in 2009. He was a music producer working with platinum hip-hop artists and producers in the industry. 45th was filled with so much life and ambition that it was a joy just to be around his electric personality. He was a walking lighthouse spreading hope. His work ethics were second to none. It's become normal to think of him when I'm working really late and into the morning sunrise. At some point and time before I stop or pass out in front of my computer, I'd often ask myself the same simple question,

"Was I being productive as possible?"

Hope you're in a peaceful place, my brother. It was a pleasure knowing your sisters and working with you since our church days growing up. Those were some great years. Thanks for the motivation, support, and years of positive energy. Miss you bro...So many of us miss you. Yes, I am making Progress! I hope you're still reading my books in peace.

Til' we meet again,

King Kevin Dorival

DEDICATION

FIRST AND FOREMOST, I'D LIKE TO THANK OUR PARents for giving birth to us. Rest in peace and power to the kindest of all angels, my mother, Queen Rosette Pierre, and my Great Aunt Jacqueline. Thank God that I was able to make it to this stage in life. A special thanks in advance to my blessing and queen, Darline Stuart, for giving birth to our first child. You're such a great woman, and I thank you for your genuine support! And to Jean W. Paul, my oldest brother, who has played a major leadership role in my life. Thank you for showing me how to be a great dad. To all my siblings, cousins, beautiful nieces, and nephews — I love ya'll. I am a super proud uncle and will do anything to encourage and support each of you to continue reaching for the stars in any way I can. It feels like we were just changing your diapers, helping with your homework, and now many of you are at the doorsteps of college. You're gods and goddesses with the genetics to excel in whatever you place your mind and faith on. To my oldest two nephews, King David and Devaughn L. Mortimer, you'll always be my first sons.

Much love to my queen mothers and brethren. Bless up to all my family and friends in Haiti, throughout Africa, the Bahamas, Florida, Georgia, Arizona, New York, and London. Thanks for buying my books and supporting my films. I hope everything I do blesses your life in more ways than one. Keep your head up, and your spirit higher. I appreciate everyone who played a role in helping me move this book forward. Lord knows it has been one heck of a ride but hey, it's finally here. I LOVE ALL OF YOU! To Principal Corey Wilson, my former Deerfield Beach High School track & field coach, you're the best coach I've ever had. And to Mrs. Sonji

Wyche, never hesitate to ask me for anything. I am the Winner In The Mirror because of you.

To all of the Nicholas Murrell's, McKenzie Adams, Ahmaud Arbery's, Bryce Gowdy's, Adam Walsh's, Michael Finn's, George Floyd's, Fredrick Allen Hampton's, Victoria Climbié's, and Sherrice Iverson's of the world—this one is for you!

Blessings Always Override Curses.

INTRODUCTION

*G*O FOR THE WIN! KNOWING YOU ARE SOMEONE GREAT requires *believing* you are great. It starts right now in this very moment by saying, "I AM someone unique, going somewhere great!" As soon as you speak those words, the consciousness of The Creator is activated within you. The timing of your actions, and the use of your mind is everything. The time is now to live your blessed life!

Taking the energy to write and share my inspirational messages with the world has been a long time coming, a dream finally made into a reality. Have you ever felt like winning and being successful is not designed for you? Almost, as if you are not worthy of the good things in life or destined to be a loser due to the fact that everything you've tried your best to accomplish flops like a broken pancake? It may come as a surprise to you, but for the first couple of decades of my life I too felt like a loser. As a child, I was verbally and physically abused by people who should have shown me the love I deserved. They misused their power and imposed their negativities on me until I believed I was nothing. I walked and talked like a loser to myself and to others. Mentally, without knowing it, I internalized becoming a failure and an underachiever. Internalize is one of my favorite words, and it's a pretty powerful one, meaning to make (attitudes or behavior) part of one's nature by learning or unconscious assimilation; also, it's defined as acquiring knowledge of.

I didn't understand why, but miraculously, deep down inside and despite my guardian's nightmarish treatment, I felt there was something awesome about myself. My imagination showed me I was a rich prince and a brave warrior in another lifetime. I knew there was a winner within, but I just couldn't see him in the mirror. When I looked at my reflection all I saw was a lame chicken instead of a glorious eagle or a powerful lion. You see, when people talk down to you in a hateful manner, they are trying to speak curses over your life by causing you to see yourself as less than, rather than greater. Verbal abuse in turn impacts your self-awareness, self-esteem, and shatters the proper inner standing of who you are to become. It isn't that they don't love you; they simply dislike themselves and have a twisted understanding of what love is. Dr. Amos Wilson labels the paradox as a "love from hate." They despise themselves for various reasons. So, to feel normal, similar to a poisonous snake, they spew all of their toxic energy onto those who they perceive as defenseless and vulnerable prey. Over time, I realized my high level of confidence was my titanium shield. The more I believed in myself, the more I was able to tune them out and tune in the universe's vibrational messages, which led me through my journey, my path of light—victory after victory. In the dark places of life, when you're confused and lost, truth and light are very useful. And knowledge of self will set you free.

It's my hope that this literary work helps to make the world a better place, one person at a time. We are living in a time where the vast majority of us are constantly forfeiting our spiritual gifts, tossing out everything but the kitchen sink! Our dignity, willpower, identity, hope, and faith in ourselves, plus other important aspects of our lives, are being thrown out with the bathwater more than ever before. You can even argue that our society has an identity crisis, especially this generation of youth, who has a record high suicide rate among them. My heart will always have a soft spot for children, the underdogs of this world, which was the catalyst that compelled me to write this book. I was once someone that contemplated suicide. I was once someone who never thought I'd win anything in life. I was once someone who couldn't see college in my future. I was once someone who believed that life wasn't fair. I was once all of those things, but now I AM MORE THAN A CONQUERER! You will be one as well. If my writing can help save one life, I'll be satisfied. However, if I can help save a thousand lives, I'll be more than thrilled!

As you read, you'll learn step by step exactly how to hold your shield of light high and your spirit even higher. The next time someone wants to give you a piece of their ugly mind, you'll be ready to deflect their negativity. This is not a book that is trying to push you to believe or not to believe in a deity, a god or God, the Creator. I'm simply sharing with the world how I freed my mind, body, and spirit., in which enable me to tap into the divine energy and power that we all have, but only a small percentage of us are conscious of.

Even as I finished the last draft of this manuscript on December 30, 2019, an old classmate's son, Bryce Gowdy, a seventeen-year-old standout senior from my old high school shocked everyone. He committed suicide by jumping in front of a freight train in Deerfield Beach, a small South Florida town that's flooded with talent. The community was left in dismay and his family was devastated. He was an All-American football star who had just received a full scholarship to Georgia Tech. Everything in our life may look good on the outside, but if we have a hurricane brewing inside, it is bound to show up in unimaginable ways.

Everyone wants to feel important, but this isn't always the case. People will create a façade to become the person they desire in the mirror. "Fake it until you make it," they say. But at what cost? Your soul? Your dignity and self-respect? If success, financial wealth, and power come with such large prices, then it isn't worth it. Case in point, many years ago, I read about a man who believed he was Jesus. He dressed up in a robe, grew his hair to his shoulders, and spoke in parables as if he were living in 880 AD. He formed his identity based on the false pale-skinned, blue-eyed, and commercial image of the Son of God that hangs on the walls in millions of churches, schools, and homes around the world. People would constantly tell him that he wasn't Jesus, but he ignored them since he rebuked them as devils in his blue eyes. Specialists from around the world visited the mental institution to treat him, but they all failed. No one had a solution until a special psychologist claimed he held the answer to snapping him out of his identity crisis, and back to reality.

The new doctor pleaded with the hospital staff to stop telling the patient that he wasn't Jesus. In his eyes, he was Jesus, which was the foundation of the problem. The way he dressed and spoke were symptoms of the problem. The more they told him he wasn't Jesus, the more defensive and offended he got, and the deeper he dug himself into his mirror of self-deception. The doctor told the staff that they had to find a way to get him to look indirectly into the mirror on his own accord. Forcing him to directly look into the mirror only caused natural resistance. It's like when our parents tried to force us to eat vegetables. Most of us resisted, but over time, we came to understand that eating vegetables is beneficial for our overall health. So, we were able to step outside of our disdain and prioritize our well-being.

In the same light, the patient had to see his true reflection in the mirror to snap out of his psychosis. The patient understood the Bible from front to back and had pretty much memorized all the scriptures, so he was clearly intelligent — perhaps missing a few marbles, but was not a fool at all. The doctor cleverly asked the patient if he could build a table since Jesus' father, Joseph had taught him carpentry. He simply could not build a table to save his life or even use the necessary tools for construction. It was at that point that he began to reconsider his reality. He was able to look into his mental mirror and wake up from his imaginary world. After that day, he never called himself Jesus again. You see, the fundamental issue wasn't his looks but his mind. He was ripe for a mental makeover but didn't know it or probably didn't recognize it until he subtly looked into the mirror. Positively reprogramming our mind beneficially changes our reality. Now, it is possible to completely focus our energy on accomplishing our dreams. Time and money are both important, however, our personal energy is often overlooked. For it is energy that makes the world go round.

The patient's situation clearly affirms the adage "Everyone is right in their own eyes." At times, we practice selective hearing by listening to what we want to hear, and block out what we don't. The gentleman had to see for himself who he really was, and at the end of the day, that's all that matters. Who do you truly see yourself as? A winner or a loser? An eagle or a chicken? Leader or a jester?

You have the power to control the narrative and choose how you carry yourself. You can talk big and portray a larger-than-life persona on social media, at church, or at work, but you have to be real with yourself. The truth of the matter is who you are is mainly determined by what you choose to do or don't with the time and space allotted to you on this planet. You are what you do, and not just who you say you are. Also, our inactions are actions that speak for themselves. Your community service is the rent you pay for the air you breathe every day on earth; this goes for the rich and the poor. What you produce with the energy you put out into the universe determines who you truly are and guides the path you take. You are the tree; the fruits you produce come from your thoughts, words, and actions. Please, stop for a quick second and think about the following question:

What type of fruit grows from your tree?

We must healthily love ourselves in order to become one with ourselves and to have a true sense of happiness. Peace, harmony, and reciprocity will flow freely and abundantly once we are able to do so. It's a beautiful thing when we are in sync with who The Creator designed us to be and not what the pressures of the world conditioned us to be.

Nevertheless, I have sensed that society is going to continue to lose faith more and more with each passing day. Today, the manner of which many of our youth carry themselves shows that they lack confidence and a zeal for life. Many of them are covering their faces with tattoos to express their frustrations and to fit in a culture of their own twisted ideology. To be honest, we have to hold the parents accountable for the direction of the mindset of their children. It seems as if a large number of parents are more interested in indulging and trolling online than actually parenting. Many of our youth aren't sure who they are outside of indulging in entertainment, their social media profiles, music, and reality TV, all of which seem to get more and more cantankerous by the day, especially in the "new normal" where it seems as though anything goes. Growing up in the 80's and 90's you'd never hear cursing on a TV program, but these days that's all we hear. Without a firm grip on reality and a sense of positive direction, it's so easy to lose yourself. It brings to mind the quote from Lewis Carroll's, Alice's Adventure in Wonderland: "If you don't know where to go, any road will take you there."

Don't get me wrong, mainstream entertainment can bring some value; you just have to know where to look and what to listen for. Back when I used to watch vampire movies, there was a creepy component about the dark bloodsuckers that stood out to me. Once someone was bitten, they were not sure if they had yet turned from the land of the living into the living dead. The first confirmation that they had transformed came when they peeked into a mirror and couldn't see a reflection of themselves. Can you imagine looking into the bathroom mirror and seeing nothing or just a fraction of your former self? That has to be one of the most horrible feelings in the world. It can only compare with being oblivious of who you are or what your life's purpose is.

Life can take us on a heavenly roller coaster or one hell of a ride. The good news is you have the power to control which direction you're heading, along with the pace. You may not be able to have full control of every aspect, but you better believe you have the choice to jump off or keep riding that train. The truth is, many of us find out too late that the ride stopped a long time ago.

Those of us from the states grew up wanting to live that good ol' American Dream of a blissful marriage with beautiful children in a big home, with a bright career, a dog, and a white picket fence. We go to college and start our own businesses in hopes of moving up that ladder of success, drafted into major sports, and providing for our family. We do all we can to chase that mighty dollar 'by any means necessary' and are obsessed with securing that bag full of cash that's heavily promoted these days. Without a doubt, many people have sold their souls in the pursuit of riches and glory. I wish it weren't true, but there have been hundreds of cases where a son or daughter killed their parents for an early inheritance. Cases like this aren't new. The greed for money and power has caused many people to commit the unthinkable to those closest to them since the beginning of time. They lost their identities and values in the cyclone of paper chasing, unable to see themselves positively again — just like the vampires. Don't become one of those types. Money isn't the root of all evil, it's the lack of values and morals that will rot the soul. Understand that good values include worthwhile things such as love, honor, dignity, courage, and respect, not greed, betrayal, money, cars, clothes, and random sexual exploits.

As a woman of honor or man of valor, it's important to know who you are. It's also vital to know where your family is from, what your ancestor's roots, victories, defeats, and cultural values are; what's expected of you for the sake of improving your lineage, and what's your genetic code comprised of? This will give you a reference point on your *M.A.P. (Must Achieve Purpose) of Life.* Without a map, while traveling you'll be lost. It will be difficult to unlock the supernatural powers (mind, body, and spirit) you were born with. M.A.P. out your dreams!

Moreover, many of us stare into the mirror and have no idea who we truly are or what we have become. We're lost due to the constant drama and self-inflicted wounds from living in a war zone with a lack of family history. El-Hajj Malik El-Shabazz, also known as Malcolm X, once said, "If you don't know who you are, then you're whatever anyone tells you that you are. We need more light on each other. Light creates understanding, understating creates love, love creates patience, and patience creates unity."

This book is designed to encourage you, the underdogs of the world, to hang on to your passions with a positive outlook. It may take every ounce of your spirit to achieve your dreams; it may take every bit of strength you can physically and spiritually muster, your last dollar, or every brain/neuro cell you have to live the best life you've envisioned. The fact of the matter is, we never really know how much we have left in the tank until it's time to use the last bit of fuel left. It's during the storms of life that we find out who we truly are. If you have a dream that has not come to pass yet, there is something to hold onto and to have hope for. Fight for what you believe in and do not throw in the towel just because everything isn't going how you envisioned it. Guess what? It rarely does. You never know if the hundredth door you've knocked on is the very one God has brought you to so you can receive the blessings prepared for you. In that moment it doesn't matter if all the other ninety-nine doors were previously slammed shut in your face.

Even though it's sometimes hard to get support or to get those you love to invest in your vision, you must not get weary. This is the very reason you should not *chase* your dreams, but rather *pursue* them. If you continue chasing that mighty dollar or that man/woman, you'll eventually get tired. On the contrary, when you're pursuing something, you're enabling yourself with the time, wisdom, and character to align with the right people according to your written plan. Perhaps, it may entail going down an unexpected route that will prove to be ten times more fruitful than you originally planned. As long as you don't mentally or spiritually give up during the marathon, remain consistent with the right attitude; if you stick to your *winning equation* you will be more than alright. Don't just be in the game, give it your best shot. GO FOR THE WIN!

WHY IN THE HEAVENS
DID I WRITE THIS BOOK?

*A*FTER I RELEASED MY AUTOBIOGRAPHY, *THE Courage to Believe: Never Give Up, Keep Moving Forward,* an inspirational story so wild and unbelievable, it's hard to believe that it was written by me. As the natural high of motivating people didn't leave my heart, the urge to write another inspirational book became engraved in my mind until I could no longer bear the burden. It felt as if hot coals were burning on top of my head signaling me to write. I simply couldn't wait to write the words that could set a countless number of people free from the prisons of their own minds and reality, in the same manner as I once had been caged in. Most people struggle to get from a concept to a manifestation, but like NASA's motto, "Failure is not an option!" In my book, neither is giving up, literally.

There will always be a fresh wind on the way to propel you to the next level of your journey, as long as you keep moving forward. For a long time, I didn't believe in myself, but something clicked in me that allowed me to snap out of that "stinking thinking". For example, the mindset of a loser that does nothing but manifests a losing reality. If you only see what you want to see, you won't see what you need to see. Everything happens for a reason, and this is your season to see the greatness you were born to be. You may not look or feel like much now, but you are stronger than you think. When the appointed time comes, you'll see the power of The Creator within you show up and show out! Why is that? As you're preparing yourself for the opportunities on their way, know that you have the favor of God buried deep inside. It is growing by the minute and waiting for you to step up to a challenge that is threatening your destiny.

Herein we are going to take a journey through the history of winning philosophies and green prints, from successful individuals. You'll also learn about the natural laws of power, and some effective methods that will enable you to break the shackles of the mind. I will share stories from some of the world's brightest minds and provide a glimpse of personal experiences that have helped me tremendously in my pursuit of excellence.

Over the years, I've spoken at churches and community organizations in different parts of the world; from the Caribbean Islands to London and throughout America. People always thought that I was a pastor, but "I AM" just an encourager, an underdog that stood up one day and fought his giants instead of running away from them. Indeed, there are levels to this, just like when a young eagle attempts to take its first flight because its confidence increases with each flap of its wings while still in the nest. Distinguished people like Queen Nzinga, General Hannibal Barca, King Henri Christophe, Shaka kaSenzangakhona (Shaka Zulu, Emperor of the Zulu Kingdom), Harriet "Moses" Tubman, General Toussaint L'Ouverture, Steve Jobs, Jack Ma, Mary Ellen Pleasant, Annie Minerva Turnbo Malone, King David, and A.G. Gaston would have never become leaders, queens, kings, pioneers, and multimillionaires if they'd chosen to run away from their calling. Their journeys weren't a walk in the park, which included many game-changing legal and bloody battles. They made history, and it's time for us to make our mark too! Why not?

People need to be inspired and reposition their souls back into their right minds and temple. With the help of this book, you are going to resurrect your dreams and zeal for life out of the graveyards of a lethargic routine. The only way to do this is to, first, find the keys to unlock the vortex to the portals of successful ideas in your mind, then you'll see ... *"The Winner In The Mirror."*

"Every great dream begins with a dreamer. Always remember, you have within you the strength, the patience, and the passion to reach for the stars, to change the world."
— Harriet Tubman

ONE STEP CLOSER

1

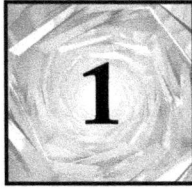

THE GOD INSIDE: YOUR INNER-G

"Ye are gods, and all of you are children of the Most High."

PSALMS 82:6

UCCESS IS AN INNER PROCESS AND NOT SOMETHING that you automatically get out of life. Triumph is something that you bring to the table. The more you learn to work your mind, the less you'll have to use your behind. In troubling times, we must move from one-dimensional thinking to three-dimensional thinking, that's thinking beyond what you can see with your physical eyes. It's above and beyond common logic and speaking analytically: thinking with your mind, body, and spirit. We're either trapped or propelled forward by the words that we speak out of our mouths into the atmosphere. As individuals, we have the choice of motivating ourselves or becoming our own worst enemy. For it is my honor and privilege to have someone as important as you are to take the time to read my scholarship and deep thoughts on enhancing your life through accumulating power, wisdom, and the goal of obtaining and maintaining a peace of mind. This book may very well be the entrance to your spiritual journey for universal love, divine wisdom, and infinite power.

People who have just undergone plastic surgery to correct a part of themselves that they hated about themselves, minds were filled with so much self-negativity that after the surgery they still couldn't see the improvement. After surgery has dramatically improved their appearance, they negate the change, refuse to acknowledge it, insist that they look the same as they did before the operation. Showing them before and after photographs does no good; it even arouses anger. Dr. Maxwell Maltz, a plastic surgeon, explains, "For people's image of themselves—good, bad, or natural—depend on past successes and failures. This concept of one's own worth is so important, so much deeper and <u>more meaningful than a mirror</u>. People carry this self-image into present activities and into plans for the future too."

The world already has more than enough negative energies, enemies, and pessimists waiting to challenge your hopes and dreams at every corner. You'll need every weapon available to fight for what is yours. Some of those weapons are readily available, while others are of the supernatural kind, and will take special methods to tap into them. The good news is that the positive forces of the universe are available to assist us. You will not find God until you first find God from within your Inner-G. Once you find the God inside of you, you'll see the divine in everybody — well, almost everybody. Let's face it, there are many devils among us and not enough angels. Still, everyone deserves love, and you cannot healthily love others if you do not love yourself first. How can you give what you don't have? The Divine Creator gave us the ability to possess faith, determination, and self-love; with these components nothing is impossible. All things are possible for those who believe. In essence, the person who believes in him or herself is a reflection of *God in action*.

When things get tough (and they most certainly will), fortify your mind with positivity by saying and believing, "This is only temporary—I can hang on. I can do it! I am on my way to a wealthy place!" People go on for years seeking some level of redemption for a mistake or a missed golden opportunity due to the fact redemption clears our conscience. It's sad to say, but many of us don't get the chance to redeem ourselves after a failed marriage, a sour business endeavor, or an awful spending habit since we wait on others to redeem us instead of taking the bold steps to redeem ourselves. It's truly an exhilarating feeling once you decide to affirm yourself.

Believe it or not, I tried my hardest to walk a straight line and stay out of trouble, but trouble kept finding me, almost as if I were a magnet for negativity. No matter how hard I worked to try and keep my nose clean, I somehow ended up being reprimanded by the system. I couldn't take Florida Atlantic University courses while sitting in jail waiting to see a judge for a non-technical (no new charge) probation violation. The process can take days, maybe even a week, which is more than enough time for anyone to flunk all of their college courses.

By the Grace of God and the praying warriors in my family, like my mother and mentors, I was able to catch up on the schoolwork that I missed. Unfortunately, the scenario occurred on two other occasions. There was even a probation officer who had the audacity to tell me, "You will not graduate from college, and you are not college material. So why even try?" She was a demon trying to provoke me to anger. Her negative energy and the verbal curse she tried to spew upon my life motivated me to prove her wrong by finally deciding to fight for my future. She had too much power and was in the right position to make a lot of lives miserable, but not mine.[1] If you've taken college or technical school courses, whether part-time or full-time, then you understand the level

[1] Dorival, Kevin, "Courage To Believe: Never Give Up, Keep Moving Forward." Pompano Beach, Sky View Creative Circle, 2015.

of studying and participation required to be successful. It takes hours of reading, typing, and lots of caffeine.

Instinctively, I immediately told her, "I *will* graduate college. I don't care what you think, or what your opinion is about me! I know I will finish!" You should've seen the look on her face. I respectively stood up for myself in her office, and it felt great! From that day forth, I was the great General Hannibal Barca staring down the Romans. I didn't wait to leave the office or allow her plague of words to have a hold on me or my life. Of course, I was too wet behind the ears to realize the spiritual significance of what had happened and how my confidence increased when I spoke those words to her—from that moment on, I took my life seriously. I used the Inner-G power within me and began to speak victories, love, and success all over my life. It is said that life begins when one knows thyself. At the time, I wasn't on the path of enlightenment, therefore, like many of us, I was lost and didn't know the capacity of my power. Her job and ill-spirit were meant to belittle people, but our job is to recognize and deflect their foul energy by contending for our destiny.

I was determined to prove to anyone that ever doubted me wrong, even some family members. It was on and popping! Jealously and negativity in my bloodline wasn't a new thing to me, so I wasn't surprised by their lack of support, since most of them never graduated from high school, owned any property, or had aspirations to become entrepreneurs. Preparing your mind and heart for disappointment makes it much easier to accept, and more importantly, it helps you focus your energy on winning and not the discouragement that comes with the territory of setbacks, missed opportunities, or failures. Even the people you love and care for will most likely doubt you. Most will not believe in your greatness until they see you on television or in a magazine. The first time my father saw me in a newspaper, he automatically thought I had died. Over the years I've come to realize that most people are naturally negative thinkers, as you will see the research that proves this theory to be a fact, in a later chapter. He didn't even bother to read the amazing headline: "20 Years Later, Student Tells 5th Grade Teacher, 'Thank You'!"

That article in conjunction with my autobiography made me an overnight celebrity among schools and libraries all over Florida's Educational System. Principals and teachers shared the article via email, which resulted in me getting booked to speak at large events at schools, educational conferences, churches, libraries, and community centers. Nevertheless, one must remain determined to defeat the odds with God on their side. If I can do it, believe you can do it too! You must put your faith in yourself and what you are setting out to accomplish with no doubts, not one iota of uncertainty. Give it your all! Convince yourself that you are on the winning side by speaking words like this into your existence: "All is well. All is working toward my good. Things are already getting better!"

On August 25, 2005, I finally broke away from the chains of my generational curses. I never caved in or gave up, and I did it! I actually did it! I knew if I could graduate college with all of the unnecessary extra drama, I could do anything with my mind made up, and with my faith intact. There is no doubt that without the drama and with the right environment that I would be able to achieve great things. I also knew that this one "V" would inspire my friends and siblings, along with their children, my future children, and future grandchildren, to go above and beyond to give their best in all they do in the spirit of excellence. Most of us, are missing real life examples of the future that we want to have; the choices are limited to criminal activity in order to become successful. Once we overcome our fears, our minds become devoid from pressure, depression, and the thoughts of being a failure. The possibilities are as endless as the stars above you. I never thought that I'd write three books, start several businesses, work for Fortune 500 companies, produce films, mentor at-risk youth, start a literacy program, and speak in front of large groups of people in different parts of the world as an international speaker. This proves that once you're committed to seeing your dreams manifest and the ball gets rolling, it's definitely going to take a lot more than hell freezing over to stop you.

Listen when you pray. The Creator doesn't need information from you; instead, you need information from The Creator, God, Allah, Jehovah, Yahweh, The Mother, The Father, Dios, The Great Spirit, and The Divine Universal Power that knows all and sees all. There's a higher spiritual force that is greater than mankind can ever be. You may have a different name for the Creator, and who you worship, but that's not the point here. You can't do the talking all of the time. This is where the benefits of prayer and meditation come into play. It pays to pay attention to your inner spirit—your intuition. That's the whole point of praying! The main goal is to seek divine guidance, knowledge, wisdom, security, and spiritual protection. It's also important to communicate with the higher power of God for instructions and confirmations. Your spirituality is the most important part of your growth and development in what type of person you are and will become; it's the state of your soul, emotions, beliefs, a mindset, and connection to the infinite. A shift in priorities allows us to embrace our spirituality in a deeper way; the materialistic goods and fame that use to be the driving force to our existence will be an afterthought. For instance, morally, you know you shouldn't purchase a half a million-dollar car until you've built a half million-dollar library or school as a gift to the community.

One of the most powerful lessons you can be taught outside of believing in yourself is honoring your commitments to yourself and to others. It's hard to keep your word to others if you can't honor or rely on your words to yourself. Keep it one hundred percent with thyself. You should be the one person you can always count on. You may think abandoning the promises you made to others is minor, but over time you'll notice that it'll reflect how easily you'll abandon your dreams and promises to yourself as well. This applies to our relationships, workouts, and business ventures. Slow down, if you must, but don't quit since that quitting energy transcends into other areas of your life. Using the words, "I'll try," is an escape clause, a polite way of saying no to yourself and friends. "I'll try" is a phrase that should not be used often if you plan to win. Because when you do, you're conditioning your brain to prepare to jump ship or take flight instead of fighting at the first sign of adversity. A drop of rain, a hint of snow, your own shadow, or even a dog barking from 1,000 yards away will have you hightailing it out of your responsibilities.

Tired of the way your life is going? Sick of wanting to give up? Commit to your life's M.A.P., then be bold and take the necessary corresponding actions to go after something worthwhile. Start small and keep your commitments to yourself for just two days. Each fulfilled obligation will empower you and make you mentally stronger; not to mention, it will also make those you care about trust you more. Once you've successfully kept your commitments expand your tasks to three days, and see where you stand from there. Continue expanding your obligations for another couple of days until you've successfully kept your word for a month, then two months, and then three months, and so on and so forth.

With the courage to believe you will overcome what has been holding up your progress. A dream delayed is not a dream denied. I repeat, a dream delayed is not a dream denied. You will become victorious. When you've been an underdog, as long as I have, you'll realize the only way is up. All that is left is the warrior spirit within that The Creator gave you to keep fighting. When your divine spirit begins to align with your physical being, watch out now! The contrast in God energy will be day and night. You're going to walk and talk differently. People will take notice of your increased level of confidence. You'll carry yourself boldly like a wild honey badger. You'll even begin to impress and compliment yourself without waiting for others to validate you. Make yourself the guest of honor at your own dinner table. Dress up nicely for yourself even when you're not going anywhere, but your home office or living room (I do this all the time). Why dress up all nice for strangers all the time and never for yourself? Think about it. The way you dress and present yourself will open or close doors in the way of your success because it speaks volumes about your character and how you feel about yourself. We only get one chance to make a first impression.

Life can ultimately silence you if you don't speak up for yourself. Your Inner-G will remain dormant as long as you allow it too, considering that you're the only one with the key that can activate it. You were given the power to achieve wealth. Go get it! You were given the power to have good health. Go get that too! You were given the power to speak life into your situations. Speak it! You were given the ability to love and be loved. We may have been given these powers, but if we don't put them into action, those gifts will wither away like a dried-up grapevine that was once fruitful. We were made to be gods over our problems, yet we allow our problems to be gods over us. You are more than a conqueror! With this mindset, there isn't much that should stress you out. You'll walk boldly as a lion towards your "issues" instead of creeping timidly like a dog with its tail between its legs.

Final Thoughts

Ask yourself: What is your heart's debt? What do you want to redeem yourself from?

Usually, the answer to the second question jumps instantly to the mind, due to the constant replays in our memory bank. We all have a past and mistakes that plague our minds like hot lava; we'll often do almost anything to keep running away from them. Think deep and put the book down for a second, if necessary. Address the problem(s) so your Inner-G can focus on your goals with a clear conscience. To function successfully under trying conditions, you must concentrate on realistic goals for which you have enthusiasm for. The enthusiasm will serve as a guiding light to keep you going when things get crazy. They will help control the conflicting thoughts that are destroying your peace of mind. You have more than enough power so GO GET YOUR DREAMS!

5 METHODS TO TREASURE THE GOD POWER WITHIN YOU (INNER-G)

- ➲ With the Divine Creator and self-love, nothing is impossible.
- ➲ Honor your word to yourself and others.
- ➲ Must recognize and deflect people with a foul spirit/energy.
- ➲ When praying, listen to your inner spirit.
- ➲ Breath, think and make sound decisions from a mindset of abundance.

2

SPEAK LIFE,
SPEAK BLESSINGS,
SPEAK INCREASE!

WHAT YOU SPEAK IS WHAT YOU GET. WHAT YOU can see is what you achieve. Our words hold the creative power of either life or death. The words that flow out of your mouth can and will be held against you in the court of life. The words you speak will either propel you forward or hold you back. Your words either activate or deactivate your motivation for achieving greatness. What you produce with the energy you put out into the universe determines who you really are. You are a tree, and the fruits you bear are produced from your thoughts, words, and actions.

How do the fruits from your tree, taste? Bland, sweet, rotten, or bitter, perhaps? The only way to produce sweet fruit and to have a fruitful life is to first love yourself so you can become one with yourself; which allows you to form a healthy union with others. Secondly, through your corresponding actions, you can reflect the good you wish to have and to be in your future. Don't hate your future, learn to love your future by creating a tomorrow worth loving by planting the right seeds today. Peace, harmony, and reciprocity will flow freely and abundantly once you're able to do so. Tomorrow belongs to you. It's a beautiful thing when you are in sync with who The Creator designed you to be and not what others want you to be. It's advantageous to be authentic, rather than synthetic. The world has plenty of the latter and not enough of the former.

The benefits of being in sync with oneself doesn't stop with just you. The blessings overflow on to those in your company and into many areas of your life, particularly, into your finances. Being broke is what many of us are accustomed to, therefore, we speak the language of Brokenness not knowing we're giving power to poverty more and more within our lives. It's both pointless and depressing to consistently remind yourself and everyone around you of what you don't have and what you can't afford. Money is clairvoyant; it can see the future. Money is a queen that likes to be treated and spoken to in a certain way to gain her favor. She will only multiply if you allow her to grow. So, until you begin to view money differently, your relationship with your finances, or lack thereof, will continue to manifest.

When you give your mind a worthwhile purpose, it will work hard at what seems like miracles to obtain your expected end. Get comfortable with declaring your life's purpose both out loud and silently to yourself. Purpose Is Power! It contains the necessary energy you need to move forward to get real-life results. Your mind will work wonders when you decide you will no longer be a loser, be broke, or disgusted and will have a disdain for poverty for that is your enemy. State your morning aspirations to The Creator in the early morning and late hours. Declare your purpose during the day and before you sleep, meditate on the good you did for others, and the good you desire to be bestowed unto you. Meditate on your business ideas and your new creations day and night. Become consumed by them and never let your thoughts waver towards negativity (thoughts of failing); they will travel throughout the day and night, and into the next.

Whether its vibrant artwork, an invention, music, or a best-selling book, you must have great, out-of-the-box ideas to break out of the rat race that society forced you in. The competition is too steep to think that being average is enough. Challenge yourself by using meaningful and larger words with fuller sentences than what's within your basic vocabulary. People who are involved with investing in diamonds, real estate, and hedge funds don't usually focus on welfare policies or Dollar Store discounts, unless they're owners; they're in an entirely different income bracket, millions and sometimes billions of dollars. Therefore, their conversations, ambitions, and thinking patterns will always differ; too much is at stake for entrepreneurs not to be on par with the competition. What type of conversations are you having with your circle? Partying, sex, harming others, committing armed robberies, and drugs, or investments, longevity, history, the future, and assets? When we speak words into the atmosphere, they set a path toward a certain direction. The next time you're with your friends and family, don't say a word and just listen attentively to the conversations. When you do so, you'll notice a pattern. Show me your friends and I'll show you your future.

Asking yourself questions and thinking of solutions has been proven to give the brain a mental workout. Just like the muscles of the body, the brain gets stronger through consistent mental (and physical) exercises and determination when it's given a task to accomplish.[2] Thinking orderly produces orderly brain chemistry and proper functioning for opening new channels, which leads to new ideas, and therefore new possibilities. By channeling such harmful thoughts like "I am sick and tired of this," "I could just kill myself," or "Would someone just shoot me," you will begin to recognize the connections between language, mental disease, and depression. In due time, with this increased awareness, you will begin to eliminate those negative thoughts and feel a change in your overall well-being.

Creativity, imagination, and other methods of cognition improve

---

[2] 22 Facts About the Brain." DENT Neurologic Institute. 2019, July 22. https://www.dentinstitute.com/posts/lifestyle-tips/22-facts-about-the-brain-world-brain-day/

the way our brains react to new concepts. Our brain is always seeking new circuitry and neural pathways in order to reward us with fruitful ideas that can sometimes, make us millionaires. We all have good ideas, and some of them are cute, however, occasionally we get an idea that is excellent. Jump on those brilliant concepts because if you don't someone else will. That is why many of us enjoy seeing the artwork in museums, engaging in interesting conversations, deep meditations, or listening to new music—we enjoy the brain-tickling feeling. The mental stimulation from these activities causes us to begin exploring new patterns and positive thoughts. Brain research by physicist Gordon L. Shaw, which is summarized in the book *Brain: The Complete Mind*, suggests listening to mind-stimulating music from classical artists, such as Mozart or Beethoven, causes a short-term increase in your ability to solve spatial problems and boosts your cognition across many levels, from simple perceptions to deeper thoughts.[3]

We are often too turnt up into the wrong type of music that is filled with violent scenes, drugs, lustful behaviors, and death. Turn it down a little bit, or even a whole lot. The mind is a canvas looking to be painted upon; it's so powerful that it only needs a fraction of a second to internalize an image, symbol, and sound. Tone down the negativity in your ears and try listening to peaceful songs regularly. Entertainment has both positive and negative narratives, depending on the spirit behind the writing, directing, and production in question. Most of us watched a movie before and felt really great about ourselves by the end of the film. While other movies had the exact opposite effect by making you feel depressed, scared, or angry, and we find ourselves scratching our head while asking, "Why in the heavens did I watch that film?" Music has the same impact on our psyche. This is why we should attempt to listen to peaceful tunes from classical, gospel, rhythm and blues, and country artists. Music is therapeutic in a sense. A few personal suggestions would be Jonathan

---

[3] Sweeney, Michael S., "Brain The Complete Mind: How It Develops, How It Works, And How To Keep It Sharp." (National Geographic, November 17, 2009)

Nelson's gospel song that has a Caribbean twist "I Believe" or "Bettah," Sade's "Sweetest Taboo," and one of my all-time favorite songs in the world, "Over the Rainbow" by the late, Israel "IZ" Kamakawiwoʻole. In my opinion, IZ's single is one of the best feel-good songs made in recent years. I listen to it to help lift my spirits up from time to time and to calm down my butterflies before most of my major public speaking events. Good music soothes the spirit and calms the mind.

Repeat after me:

"I *am* ready and willing to breakout into greater success, higher heights, and prosperity. Money is coming to me from the north, east, west, and south! Money and prosperity will follow me. I'm in agreement that money and prosperity are chasing me down! Money is my friend and not the enemy. I *am* making money while I sleep and as I eat. I, [add your name here], *am* a future multi-millionaire."

The mind must always be conditioned in some fashion. It's either you do it consciously with good thoughts and intentions, or the powers that be will cleverly increase their herd of sheep marching headfirst to the slaughterhouse, as can be seen in today's prison industrial complex. And even worse, some evil degenerates will take advantage to force whatever agenda they have in store for you. So, I'd say make up your mind that you're going to invest in yourself because you deserve the best, and nothing less. We tend to spend a significant amount of time and money, especially men, to prove to women how much money we have and strong we are. When we finally reach both—we want more of it.

Prove it to yourself first that you are great and win over your mind by giving it strict orders to focus on the good and genuine love you have in your life. Take the energy to appreciate the simple things. If you don't, the world will keep reminding you of what you don't have; this will make you feel lost, confused, and will cause you to be vulnerable to being easily manipulated into accepting lies as truths and truths for lies, which is all geared to keep the masses thinking and acting in a backwards fashion. If you don't change your mindset, the world will program it for you. Your mind will be targeted with subliminal messages through marketing scare tactics and propaganda to do anything and everything under the sun that's opposite of the good you want for yourself, your purpose, and your destiny.

Adolf Hitler's brainwashing of the German people is a perfect example of how propaganda can amazingly be used to program the minds of an entire country. In Hitler's regime, Nazi Propaganda Minister Joseph Goebbels, once said, "If you tell a lie big enough and keep repeating it, people will eventually come to believe it." He calls this war strategy, "The Big Lie" technique. If you think this method has stopped since the end of World War II on September 2nd, 1945, then you're sadly mistaken—it has never ceased. When other people control you, it's usually to get you to act or spend money frivolously to your own demise and for their benefit. This leads to a life of hell on earth (i.e., poverty, death, incarceration, and self-destructive behavior). Many of us have been told for years that we are dumb, stupid, poor, and whatever else, so why not flip the script? You have the power to control the narrative. We all should constantly channel our minds to zero in on what's worthwhile such as health, wealth, happiness, finding true love, birds singing in the trees, dolphins leaping out of water, and prosperity. How? View your mind as a TV or radio with multiple stations playing all at once. Choose one, the "I Believe In Me" channel will brighten up your years. Block out of all the other stations and focus on this channel.

Start speaking this to yourself, confidently and joyfully:

"I AM the master of my fate, faith, and the captain of my soul!"
"I AM the master of my fate, faith, and the captain of my soul!"
"I AM the master of my fate, faith, and the captain of my soul!"

How our mind absorbs, accepts, and rejects information should not be taken lightly. It's invigorating to be able to control your destiny, dance to your own rhythm, and not being forced to jump up and down like a (corporate) slave. You set the terms when you're an entrepreneur and the master of your fate. We determine how much we want to be paid based on the amount of time and sweat equity that we have invested in our business. It feels great meeting your clients at a mutual time to pick up your check! Being independent is an incredible experience that entrepreneurs thrive on. Self-possession, means, "the state of or feeling of being calm, confident, and in control of one's feelings." It's a must for any entrepreneur to have self-possession, since majority of the deals are made on the basis of a confident aura. It takes confidence to launch out on your own; there's a reassurance that everything will be okay when you love the person that you see in the mirror. In this case, no one is controlling your rhythm—you are!

European Time and African Identity

Dr. Amos Wilson, a Pan-African thinker, scholar, and psychologist, wrote a lot of mind-blowing information in his extraordinary book, Black-On-Black Violence: The Psychodynamics of Black Self-Annihilation in Service of White Domination. Dr. Wilson, did a remarkable job in explaining how our ability or inability to control our time and rhythm creates the quality of life (space) we live in. "To be an African living under European domination is to live in a time-warp; to live out of sync and is therefore tantamount to living in a state of false consciousness. To know one's time is to know oneself. To know one's rhythm and to live in accord with it, is to live harmoniously and healthy. To live by running against the grain on one's time, to live according to another's time, is to live anemically and maladaptively. It is to be enslaved by one's timekeeper—to live for him, and not for oneself. This is the African situation.

Having been removed against their will from their continent, the Africans have been denied access to their own self-generated time and rhythm means by which time reveals itself to consciousness … evolutionary infrastructures of their minds, bodies, consciousness, social relations, social organizations, desires, and identities." [4]

Speaking of rhythm, time, and space, you may know him as Louis Armstrong (August 4, 1901, to July 6, 1971), but I know him as "Satchmo". He was the famous jazz musician that rocked the world from the 1920s to the 1960s. Armstrong had an interesting perspective on life's rhythm. He made up a very creative term for those that are in command of their time as being *rhythmmatical*, which he defines as being in sync with your time and space and perfectly aligned with the energy of those around you. Mr. Armstrong credits his success as a musician, husband, and personal life on his *rhythmmatical skills*. A person that does not control their time, rhythm, and space isn't in control of their life at all. You can't always choose the music life plays but you can choose how to move to it.

One must start by awakening, acting upon, and embracing the god within, then all the powers The Creator possesses will be yours. All of it! Acknowledge the architect of the heavens, the earth, the ocean, the animals of the land and sea, women, men, and children. This is an immense amount of power you've always had access to but was thrown off rhythm by the storms of life. Your power must be willed into reality from both your conscious and subconscious mind, which certainly does take practice and patience. In a later chapter, we will go over how to do just that.

Growing up, my mother was the lead singer in our church's choir.

[4] Dr. Wilson, Amos. Black-On-Black Violence: The Psychodynamics of Black Self-Annihilation in Service of White Domination. New York City, Afrikan World InfoSystems. First Edition. 1990

She was a singing champion! It was inevitable that my siblings and I would spend countless hours in church. We memorized many of the miraculous stories of the Bible from an early age. Over the years, I've heard many iterations of them from different pastors with their interesting perspectives and with people from all walks of life. I've listened attentively to most of the rhetoric from the reverends in the pulpit to jailhouse pastors and drunken wise men under the shade tree. Fortunately, the paradigm shift in my faith happened when I was forced to apply spiritual lessons to real-world situations through tangible actions with my God-given abilities. It's not enough to just feel good and to have goosebumps. Emperor Napoleon Bonaparte, is known for his inspiring quotes, and this one doesn't disappoint, "Take the time to deliberate, but when the time for action has arrived, stop thinking and go in."

We have more than enough religions in our lives, so it's time to make some power moves and real money (hundreds of thousands to millions). There is no time like the present to use your mind power! Purposely push yourself to obtain God's consciousness, knowing the god in you is the source of <u>divine and infinite intelligence</u>. There is no need to be worried about anything because your Inner-G will guide you in everything. With divine infinite knowledge, wisdom, and good intentions, anything is possible. Without God, I *am* nothing. With God, I *am* everything!

By acknowledging, the great "I AM" you'll also recognize the god (the beauty and power) in others which will cause a ripple effect of love, respect, and ultimately, a more peaceful and harmonious world. The ancient principles of Ma'at were a way of life, and still is amongst the conscious community. Their principles kept individual relationships and the populace in check without the enforcement of a government. It gave ancient high-culture civilizations boundaries to live by and helped improve the Law of Reciprocity among them. The Law of Reciprocity is a Universal Law that says when someone does something nice for you, there will be a naturally deep-rooted psychological urge to do something nice for them in return. There are thousands of people that practice the principles of Ma'at today, including me.

Here are several Ma'at principles that will be a blessing to your life:

1. I have not committed sin.
2. I have not committed robbery.
3. I have not told lies.
4. I have not made anyone cry.
5. I have not stolen from a God or Goddess.
6. I have not polluted the water.
7. I have not cursed a God or Goddess.

From the few principles I've shared out of the forty-two, you can see that the followers of Ma'at had a level of awareness about their actions that we must implement in our troubled society today to some degree. Do any of those principles sound familiar? The biblical Ten Commandants derive from the forty-two principles of Ma'at. The ancient civilization of Kemet viewed themselves as gods having a human experience. Your Inner-G automatically prepares you to rule and reign in your world. The rest is up to you. Life becomes golden when we treasure our divinity and precious energy. The next time you're faced with a stressful situation, instead of turning to the Google gods or pulling out your hair, activate your Inner-G. Don't waste your time and energy messing around with petty situations and people, or allow life's most special moments to pass you by. More than anything, difficult times have shown us how quickly things can go from bad to worse. Carpe diem. Seize the day! Follow your heart.

Say these words out loud:

"God in me, please tell me what to do about this situation."

Remember, that your tongue holds life, death, prosperity, or poverty. The positive words you speak will produce positive outcomes when you put love, kindness, and the necessary energy into the universe. You'll be amazed at what you can do when you get the "buts," "would've," "should've," and could've," out of your way. In some cultures, those words don't even exist. It's either you did it or you didn't. When it comes to your goals in life and those that you love, it behooves you to trash all of those words; replace them with "I will," "I can," and "I am!"

On the contrary, the portal of hell leads to a gloomy world [immense negativity, pain, and suffering] unleashed into your life when you spew cantankerous and foul words and sentences out of your mouth. These destructional words are, in turn, fed to your subconscious mind, perpetuating the negativity in your life—no one wants that. Reflecting on your past can be a great thing when it involves great memories and valuable lessons. Nonetheless, there's a caveat: if all you are doing is holding onto past memories, you'll be locked into an old-time capsule, unable to create new victories, new memories, or the future you desire.

The only thing better than an old victory is a new one. *Can I get an Amen?* Even though the smiles of the past can last a lifetime, you have the power to create a new future. Everything that is written has the ability to be spoken. You have the God-given ability to speak life and blessings into your life. Your enemies don't want that though. Your enemies' goal is to keep you silent and stagnant. I'm all for quietness, peace, and tranquility. In fact, the ability to control the noise levels in your living space, the temperature, the energy of the atmosphere, and decor is a sign of power, while an inability to control these components is the sign of a lack thereof. Too much silence makes your place feel like a mortuary, a breeding ground for depression and feelings of inadequacy, guilt, and who knows what else. All of which will push us directly into mental illness with a brand new straightjacket. Don't be silent in the face of a battle! Be defiant in your praise to the Most High! Believe in yourself, regardless of what the situation looks like or who doesn't support you.

The harsh reality is that there are lots of people that are weak-minded and extremely sensitive, and these are the kinds of people who pray for your failure and downfall every day. I personally know a few people who follow me online and 'like' many of my pictures, but that's as far as their support goes. Not even a compliment after ten years of events, books, and community endeavors. I couldn't help but think, *"Why don't they support me outside of 'text support'?"* Presuming that you're old-school like me, you'd want to see people, laugh with them, and hug them in person. Speak life to your circle in real life, as much as possible like that oldie but goodie song by Tammi Terrell and Marvin Gaye says, "Ain't nothing like the real thing, baby!"

Here are a couple of questions for you: When was the last time you gave yourself a compliment, a pat on the back, or told yourself, "Good Job?" If the people around you are cheap with their compliments, but spend lavishly on criticisms then you must, by all means, give kudos to yourself. When was the last time you took a look in the mirror and said to yourself, "Wow, I look great?" If it's been a while, do it now. Go ahead. The next time you experience a challenge, whether it's money troubles or a rocky relationship, use the power of a compliment. Say to yourself, "Wow, I'm glad I overcame that!" Better yet, tell a loved one, "We are going to overcome this!"

By speaking such powerful words of affirmation, you're pushing your spirit forward. You'll instantly feel a little better about the situation and will be in a better position to move on with your head held high with a clearer mind. It's hard to think clear when the mind is bogged down with multiple high-level problems. The truth of the matter is we rent out too much free space in our brains to our problems and people that we can't stand in our presence. Similar to how people can speak life and success into you, they can most definitely speak death as well. Many people allow the derogatory images and words placed upon them by society and the media and now social media to dictate their identity and self-worth based on the Joneses. This is a no-go. Fixate your eyes on the prize [your dreams on your M.A.P.] and not your bills or growing debt. It is far more beneficial to internalize a self-image of success than a self-image of failure. The issue here is that most of us have no idea that we've consumed a self-image of failure, therefore won't address it until it's too late. Let's be proactive about changing this, for once and for all.

In Genesis, the good book says, "Let there be light." Aren't you a god yourself? Speak light into your life, especially in those dark spaces. Speak blessings. Speak increase. Speak abundance. Speak overflow. Speak the way you want your life to be. Be as intentional as possible. The best part is that it's absolutely free. Your intentions have the same amount of power as your purpose. By allowing waves of curse words to come out of your mouth, you allow them to seep into your heart to create a tsunami of problems to crash unto the shores of your doorsteps since they were already brewing in your mind. Then, you'll become totally consumed with those harsh words and images, thereby increasing your chances of living a life plagued with death and destruction. Without even knowing it, you'll increasingly begin to think and live negatively, ultimately slowing down your progress and becoming obsolete. Life will greet you the way you greet it.

Think about this question for a quick second. How do you approach your days and greet people in the morning hours? Does your "Good Morning" come with a warm smile and zeal, or is it just a simple "morning" or a head nod? When people greet me with a "morning," "morn," or "gm" text, in my mind, I'm thinking, "You suck!" But when people greet me with a "Good morning, hope all is well," I usually reply with an exuberant, "MORNING BLESSINGS! This Is A Great Day To Be Alive! How are you doing?" See the difference in energy?

Back when I worked a nine to five, every day on my way to my office (and past jobs), I knew who I could and couldn't say good morning to. When you can't do something as simple and positive as a morning greeting to someone, then there is a serious underlining issue. For example, I used to work with a young woman who was a heavy coffee drinker and cursed like a pirate at the office. She wasn't a bad person (I like to give people the benefit of a doubt), but for some reason, for the first couple of weeks, every time I'd greet her, she'd give me this "up yours" look. Overtime I ascertained that she was in a physically abusive relationship when she came to work with a black eye and broken arm; the toxic energy from her home transcended into the workplace. When she finally broke free of that relationship she was a brand-new person with a bright smile every morning. When we say "good morning" it's to brighten up the day and bless our environment. It's a perfect way to greet the world and to compliment everyone we come across. For some folks who are troubled in their spirit, it's hard to accept that being greeted with a "good morning" or "good afternoon" is a blessing, and an indirect compliment.

Have you ever been out networking, passing out flyers or business cards, and noticed how some folks are glad to accept your material(s) while others are grouchy? People may give you an ugly look with their faces all mushed up. If you're lucky, they may throw the flyer back at you or even curse you out. You just never know what to expect when dealing with the world; therefore, you should always pray over yourself, your spouse, and your children before leaving your home. Mental prayers are great too. You can always pray in your mind, and you'll hear yourself better. Praying while meditating is very soothing. People don't always have to know what you're praying about. And for pointers, telling someone that you're praying for them is one of the best compliments you can give. You'll receive an automatic smile and their gratitude 98% of the time.

Years before I became a marketing director for a Fortune 500, international company in Atlanta's affluent Buckhead district, there was a long journey prior to earning nearly a six-figure salary. I had to pass out thousands of flyers on the streets and work on dozens of websites to get my marketing company name out there. My shorts to suits journey started my career by distributing flyers and other promotional materials for small and midsize businesses for chump change. My cousins and business partners, Gary Pierre and Even Alcime, along with some hired help, all have been chased by dogs, yelled at, and rained on more times than I can remember. It was really taxing on our bodies walking up and down the streets going from door to door in the hot South Florida sun. Truth be told, I disliked trespassing and walking door-to-door, but in my heart of hearts, I knew that it was necessary to do the dirty work. Sometimes you have to crawl through the crap before you can smell the roses. Yes, I paid my dues and will not be surprised when I become a multi-millionaire. To be honest, with my beautiful mind and heart for the people, I'll be surprised if I don't become a billionaire since I'm spiritually wealthy. You probably feel the same about yourself.

Some people found it strange, but I miss praying over the door handles of the new homes that were being built. I knew one day it would be my turn to have one built from the ground up. It was my way of visualizing a big payday that would allow me to one day own a home as beautiful as theirs. It was an exhilarating experience daydreaming about how I would decorate the place with new and exotic furniture, paintings, and sculptures. One of the homes had an impressive large mahogany Paris glass and metal double front doors with a yellow brick road as their driveway. In the center of the driveway, there was a dolphin waterfall with water shooting out of its mouth.

Eventually, years down the road I became a rare art collector and dealer. Henceforth, to make consistent income every day, I started Sky Clean Air Services, LLC., a full-service cleaning company in Atlanta. In the beginning it was just carpet cleaning for homes and businesses; that escalated into pressure washing the exteriors of homes. As calls began rolling in for different cleaning requests, we incorporated disinfecting properties by removing viruses, bacteria, and mold. On occasions, I am able to get my clients to purchase an art piece from my collection. When COVID-19 hit I went into panic mode, which forced me to rely more on my connections with The Creator and family. From there I invested a couple of grand that I received from the stimulus package to attend a six-day course to get my certified technician license in mold mitigation and water removal to expand the company's services. It's bothersome to know that most of us just sit on our money to pay bills, or to drink our lives away instead of investing in something that will increase our financial status in the near future, if not, immediately. It all started with a will, prayer, and imagination. The 'way' to make it happen became evident once I did my part by becoming a willing participant in my own success.

Instead of speaking death or hell into your world, replace it with the positive vibrations of life and love. Your words are an indication of your attitude and how far you will go in life. For example, instead of saying, "I had one hell of a day," try saying, "I had one heaven of a day!" Our positive words carry a certain frequency that opens the vortex to the life we want and desire. Pessimistic attitudes and cantankerous words don't have the voltage needed to catapult you forward. With them you might as well walk with a ball and chain tied to your leg. <u>Blessings always override curses.</u>

CHICKEN WORDS VS. EAGLE SHOUT CHART

	Chicken Words	Eagle Shout
1.	I never have enough money. I'm always broke.	I have more than enough money. I'm blessed to be a blessing.
2.	It's going to be one hell of a day.	It's going to be one heaven of a day!
3.	I can't do it! I'm going to fail. It's not going to work out.	I can do it! And I will be successful. It's going to work out just fine!
4.	It's raining outside. This suck.	It's raining blessings. Plus, I get a free carwash.
5.	I seem to always lose. I've tried this before.	I'm going to win this time! I'm going to give this my best effort!
6.	I will fail this test—it's too hard.	I studied and will pass this test with flying colors!

7.	I will never get married.	I'm one step closer to having a happy marriage!
8.	There's no reason to even try. I'm such a failure.	I'm going to give it my best shot. I'm going to be successful.
9.	I think I can but there are doubts in my mind.	I know I can! There is no doubt about it.
10.	If it weren't for bad luck, I wouldn't have any luck at all.	My luck is bound to turn around in my favor today!

Final Thoughts

Speak life, speak blessings, and speak increase. Avoid speaking and spending time on anything and anyone that goes against your vision. They'll cause you to use words and put into motion actions things that are disempowering to you and to those around you. Don't give up on yourself or your dreams. Keep your eyes on the prize, which is the future you desire. Redemption may take years to obtain, but once you do, you'll feel at peace and exhilarated.

6 Ways to Acknowledge & Activate Your Inner-G

- With the Divine Creator and self-love, nothing is impossible.
- Love and forgive thyself. [It's an exhilarating feeling of freedom.]
- Recognize and deflect foul spirits from others. Don't entertain their energy.
- When praying, it pays to pay attention to your inner spirit. Listen.
- Pray with the confidence of an eagle and not a chicken. Be bold in your prayers.
- Note what you have power of and don't. Make the proper adjustments.

SECRET STEPS
TO SUCCESS

A RENEWED MINDSET WILL GIVE YOU EVERY-
thing needed to accomplish the positive visions that
you have for your life. First, you must learn how to open your spiritual
eyes and ears to capture the messages from the universe being sent to
you with crystal clear clarity. The clearer your plans are, the easier they
are to accomplish. Why? You're equipping yourself to write a detailed
strategy that makes sense—it's easier to follow a plan that resonates with
you. To have an understanding of a matter, you have to know its defini-
tion. A favorable outcome must be defined according to what you envision. Many of the secrets to life aren't really secrets at all, especially in
regards to becoming successful. The answers are hidden in plain sight.

We can all be successful parents, farmers, astronauts, dog trainers,
and even teachers by keeping our minds intact and not all over the place.
Having the right state of mind enables you to go forth with the actions
needed to achieve your goals. The wrong state of mind results in opening a bad can of worms that will hold you back from winning. There are
even those who have reached a level of success at being couch potatoes,

THE WINNER IN THE MIRROR

ruining their reputation and even sabotaging other people's dreams as well as their own. It's all based on what you programmed your mind to see, believe, and achieve.

There are tons of blatant knowledge we think is hidden because many times, we refuse to read or listen to sources outside of our biased traditions, newspapers, social media, or religious dogmas. It's both sad but funny to know that there are people still stuck in their mindsets, who refuse to be open to new possibilities even though their spirit is screaming for change. It's possible to be born into wealth, but no one is born into success—it has to be earned—there are levels to it. There are cultural traditions, street rules, and codes that have been around for generations in every civilization. There are people that live and die by them. There are also rules and laws of manifestation that have been practiced for hundreds of thousands of years in Africa's ancient Egypt (formerly known as Kemet prior to colonization).[5] This civilization understood the laws of manifestation and tapped into the power of their brain, heart, words, and the correct corresponding actions to achieve the goals they reached.

Most of us convince ourselves that there is no need to dream of better days because our hard-knock life is constantly under siege with nothing but inevitable variables like stress, poverty, violence, and drama. In this predicament, our positive energy is usually misdirected to unnecessary situations that eat up our valuable time, money, and resources. Similar to the Law of Diminishing Return, if something isn't done to remove the negative factors to increase your quality of life, it will continue to follow the downward path until there is nothing left. It's impossible to win this way.

The first step to success is loving thyself; the second is to genuinely love others. What is wealth if you can't share your achievements with those who unconditionally love you? And if you've been fortunate enough to reach most of your goals, you shouldn't feel guilty for being

---

[5] Dr. Ivan Van Sertima, Black Women of Antiquity. Rochester: Transaction Publishes, 1998, 34.

triumphant. Eventually, I concluded that I wouldn't share my dreams and aspirations with just anyone. The decision to use discernment when choosing who to let into my world was a critical one. Back in medieval times, people would "knock on wood" in an attempt to block out unwanted ears (including demonic spirits) when they shared their dreams, goals, and secrets with someone. Why? They were afraid the wrong ears would hear them and deliberately sabotage their plans or kill them before their dreams could manifest. At the time, malevolent spirits were a real fear that paralyzed people's hopes and dreams because, in many cases, they dwelled on their fears and naysayers more than their faith and supporters.

Truth be told, most people can't handle your bigger-than-life dreams; that's why they were entrusted and given specifically to you. There would be no Michelangelo had he listened to his father to stop dreaming of becoming an artist. He followed his heart and kept drawing even though his father would beat him for it. In Italy, during the 15th Century, artists were low on the totem pole, and were looked down upon. Nevertheless, Michelangelo, with his unparalleled talent and taste for greatness, would go on to become, arguably, the greatest artist of his time. Centuries later we are still in awe at the details of his artwork, such as the *Pietà* and the fresco painting on the ceiling of the Sistine Chapel entitled, The Last Judgment, in Vatican City. None of this would've been possible if Michelangelo didn't step forward in securing Domenico Ghirlandaio, as his art mentor to guide his young artistic energy and the hunger to master his craft.

Your goals are too big for most of the folks from your childhood circles to comprehend unless you were born with a silver spoon. Now you can bless yourself with a set of silverware and everything else you desire. It's a fact of life that many will resent you when you're moving forward and they aren't. For some strange reason people often get the notion due to their negative way of thinking that your success equates to their failure. The internet has made this issue even worse because your haters can hide behind their likes. There have been cases of people being killed by jealous friends and family members. The most recent that comes to mind was in 2019 with two longtime female friends that were also coworkers. One was jealous because her best friend received a promotion at work, so she decided to take her life by inviting her over for dinner and poisoning her food.

The second step to success is to share your visions, passions, and talents with like-minded, honorable people who are aiming for a higher level of success or already reached the mountain top. Eagles do not fly with chickens, crows, or ducks; in fact, they get eaten by the Ruler of the Skies. Besides, chickens can't even fly. You'll automatically aim higher and think bigger when you are surrounded by visionaries. In the business world, where you have to network and rub elbows, it's about *who* you know and not as much about *what* you know that gets you to the table. Inside connections and friendships can be quite rewarding when it comes to securing business deals with steep competition.

A collection of brilliant minds is much more powerful than a solitary one. This was evident during and after the Reconstruction Era (1863–1877), right after the American Civil War ended in 1865. During this time, the country had an unprecedented emergence of highly intelligent black scholars, scientists, and inventors who would often put their heads together (*meeting of the minds*) to create solutions in a highly racist country. When the gun smoke cleared, leaders emerged from the ashes. These leaders included Frances Ellen Watkins Harper, Booker Taliaferro Washington, William Monroe Trotter, Marry Ellen Pleasant, Ida B. Wells, Carter G. Woodson, W. E. B. Du Bois and so many other unsung leaders who were the quintessence of unity, race pride, and intelligence. They set an unmatched precedence of excellence that continues to be mimicked today in both educational and business institutions all over the globe. They had no choice but to utilize the connectivity of their brilliant minds to elevate the Negro race out of love for themselves, their community, and for the future generations that would stand on their shoulders, such as you and I. It's a great idea to team up with like-minded people—four hands on the plow are better than two. You can run fast by yourself, but can reach further with someone else. Teamwork makes the dream work!

You deserve success the same way you deserve to have love in your life. Love has the undying power to edify, motivate, grow, and glow, thereby making the world illuminate. The opposite of love isn't hatred, it's fear. People fear what they don't understand, and through their misunderstanding, they begin to develop anger like weeds in a rose garden. Pruning your garden of the old dying leaves is essential in order to allow the new growth to capture the sunlight and much-needed nutrients from the soil. The same concept applies to our negative ideas, friends, and habits that need to be trimmed out of our minds. Let's attentively work to replace those weeds with great seeds of hope, and determination to achieve the good you deserve, the finances you want, and the people you wish to bless. Those that loathe their lives will be unable to bear the fact that you'll surpass them even though it's inevitable since you're consistent at "minding your business" and they're minding everyone else's business but their own.

On the other hand, fear has the power to do one of two things. One outcome is that it'll motivate you to overcome the situation. Secondly, it can shrink your internal bright light, your confidence, and slowly destroy everything good about you. Fear can and will eradicate everything you've worked hard for and you'll be forced to watch it all erode away. Hate has the strength to cause you to lose yourself, your composure, and self-respect as your identity goes up in smoke. Both love and fear are extremely powerful energies we can either feed or starve. Again, this is a choice you need to make, which leads me to the third step of success, which is defining what success looks like to you.

It's interesting to note that if you experience long periods of stress, depression, or anxiety, the amygdala, sometimes called the "seat of emotion," the area of the brain connected with fear and emotion, starts to shrink. This physical change in the brain structure directly affects the prefrontal cortex, which is associated with our superior brain functions like awareness, concentration, and decision-making. This proves that moments in your life will either strengthen your brain muscles or weaken them, which directly impacts how you see the world and value yourself. As a matter of fact, our experiences literally impact our brain physically by altering its size and weight. We have the mechanism to make our heart and brain 'speak' to each other to change our emotions and reduce our *Code Red* fears. This is perfect for those suffering from anxiety attacks.

Make those special moments in your life count since they most certainly will. The last thing you'd want to do is run from the challenges, hard times, and those long roads that come with life. Though it may seem like ducking and running are always the best logical options, they are certainly not and will cause more harm than good in the long run. These challenges contain within them life-defining moments. The trajectory of your life will be based on how you dealt with the great challenges before you. Consistently attempting to escape them will have a long-lasting, negative impact on your character now and your ability to win in the future; you'll program yourself (the brain's amygdala) to take flight instead of fight (stand your ground) whenever opposition presents itself. Besides, those hardships add key ingredients that you must have to design your own winning equation. No one can create this for you in view of the fact that in order for your winning equation to work, it has to be self-made and acted upon by you. Adversity leads to prosperity! In life, there are things you can pay for or pray for, but at the end of the day, you must go through challenges in order to grow.

The great obstacles you're facing are only present because you have an even greater destiny. If you were weak and had no purpose, there wouldn't be any adversity or haters devising plans to ruin you. It's all part of the pruning process. In the beginning, it will be hard to face your foes: fears, self-doubt, ghosts, and demons. I guarantee that once you take a step forward to fight your enemies, your assertiveness will grow. When you do achieve the victory, the rewards will be long-lasting; all the while your confidence will continuously increase. You will leave a necessary, positive mark on your mind and spirit, besides winning is great for morale! The amazing part is that the generations to come after you will reap the benefits. Tough times don't last, tough people, do!

"Challenges make you discover things about yourself that you never really knew."
CICELY TYSON

Make the conscious decision to starve hate and feed love into your life. Eat love until you're spiritually obese and overflowing with it. Making a clear decision is the first step in getting what you want. Stop feeding your ugly past and bad habits. Sometimes this may require you to get out of your own way and direct your attention elsewhere. Every time you focus your energy on the people and experiences from your hurtful past, you resurrect the pain and bad memories from the dead. There's no way you can achieve redemption or success if you're constantly reinvesting in events from your past. This isn't to say you shouldn't deal with unfinished business from years before. Perhaps you were betrayed or a victim of an awful crime. You have to choose to be a victor and not a victim. If that is the case, press charges and slay that demon in court. There are thousands of people who have moved on with their lives and are functioning just fine as wives, husbands, fathers, mothers, and CEOs of major corporations as if nothing happened while still carrying their pain. Many of those who are successful in those roles were able to find success because they dealt with issues and overcame past traumas. Successful counseling and a solid support base have helped countless people in this regard tremendously.

Therefore, it's essential to go back and shut those dark doors you ran away from since that experience will continue to rent space in your mind, spirit, dreams, and possibly your soul, rent-free on the condition that you don't fight back. <u>You have to get your soul back in your temple, do so by any righteous means necessary.</u> I know it's much easier said than done. Nonetheless, it must be done, even if you need someone you trust to pray and walk beside you for added strength. Every battle isn't meant to be fought alone. Whether you're aware of it or not, we consciously fertilize the things that hurt us by refusing to address them, and if we're not careful, we'll drown our future dreams with our past. Most of our battles are caused by our inability to move on and simply let go as if we're addicted to the hurt. It's nearly impossible to let go of something that we haven't address appropriately. I'm here to reveal to you the empowering tools you're already blessed with to ensure that you don't hold unto to them any longer. Invest in your future; the ROI is so much sweeter!

"If you want to be lifted up, lift someone else up!"
BOOKER T. WASHINGTON, *UP FROM SLAVERY*

Even when you can't see the winner within yourself, help someone else see their greatness, especially those who you know are doing their best to thrive. Through volunteering in community service opportunities, I learned the secret key to unlock my redemption was in supporting others, especially students, who had a burning desire to become someone great. When I first started my mentoring mission in college, I stumbled upon a valuable gem that is rare in our narcissistic society, which is servitude. It was through mentoring and helping the high school students with their studies at afterschool programs and helping in food giveaways that I completely forgot about my bones of contention. At the time, I didn't know much and could've spent my free time complaining about being homeless, hospitalized after a vicious attack, or fighting to get my college degree. The good thing is that I was smart enough to know that I didn't have the energy to waste. I kept reminding myself that I was … One day closer. The experience humbled me, and I was so thankful for what I did have: a car to sleep in, free showers at the beach, and a part-time job at Red Lobsters that allowed me to have food to eat. Their Cheddar Bay biscuits were so delicious!

At the time, I was having legal issues, my grades were dropping from a 3.35 GPA to barely a 2.0 GPA. My body became numb to the pain as I was completely lost, wanting to give up so badly. My mind was clogged with doubts and countless things that had nothing to do with the future I envisioned for myself. Once and for all, I got back into the right state of mind, I realized that my dreams are goals with a lifeline, not a deadline, and would no longer live by the system's rules. If I was going to win it had to be on my terms not XY and Z.

The mission became simple—graduate college and start a business. This would triumph would empower me to control my destiny. Walking across that stage was the oldest and most desirable dream I had since elementary school. Back in those days, I was inspired by several movies and television series like Family Matters, Good Times, The Fresh Prince of Bel-Aire, The Cosby Show, and A Different World. Today's selection of shows for children is frightening, even the cartoons aren't safe anymore with their X-rated content. Finishing my education would be the start of my success path. Inside there was a deep desire that this mission, this defining moment of my life was going to end with a V! My future depended on it and I knew it. There were no if's, and's, or but's about it. Everything was on the line. I picked up my spear and shield, and happily chose to fight! No army goes to war without a battle plan; therefore, I wrote down a few plans to keep my focus razor sharp. There was no room for errors.

In which leads me to make a request. Please, put down this book this very second and create a simple plan. Take a minute to write a couple of them down on a clean sheet of paper, which represents a clear mind. Some plans will start off as small and you're allowed to make incremental changes for the first couple of days—it's your world. Soon you'll increase the size of your goals, and your consciousness will grow along with it to help with what you've set forth to accomplish. Be sure to determine a date for your dreams to be completed and call them "lifelines" instead of deadlines. Everything around you should speak of life and not death. In a capitalistic society we're conditioned to add extra pressure on ourselves in the rat race for more cheese, and for what? Lifeline is the new way of thinking. In due time, you must expand the level of complexity of your goals. Chicken brain thinking is over! It's time to fly and I do mean fly. Reach for the stars because if you don't get there, at least you'll land on the moon with a pocket filled with stardust. Cast your net out as far as you can imagine and broaden your horizon!

GOAL GETTERS ARE EXPERTS IN GOAL FISHING

1. Create a double-sided goal list:
    Short-term (next couple of days or weeks)
    Long-term (next month, in five years, or etc.)

2. Write a couple of goals down on each side.
3. Expand your net and think bigger.

   For example, instead of eating at your favorite restaurant, set a goal to purchase your favorite restaurant.
4. Decorate your home with Feng Shui principles:

   Colors and art (see Ch. 9).
5. Meditate on your goals day and night. The more times the merrier.
6. Dream about your goal(s) by replaying it 5-10 times on your "I Believe In Me" channel before you go to sleep.
7. Practice S.B.E. (Speak it. Believe it. Execute the plan.)

It all starts by intentionally planting seeds today. Even if your faith is as small as a mustard seed, plant something positive you can look forward to in the future. An anticipated future makes life worth living. A farmer knows that in order to have a harvest, she has to plant specific seeds. That's not all, however. A successful farmer also knows that the seeds must receive water, sunlight, and a little TLC. The intentional care works exactly the same with our brains. We must mentally flush out the mental debris clogging up our minds from thinking clearly with the influx of negative experiences and detrimental thoughts. How? Simple. By supplanting them as often as possible with positive images and ideas for success. Positive in, positive out. One cost-effective way is to invest in yourself by reading edifying books from experienced people within your field of interest. Successful people possess key information and experiences from their mistakes and victories that we can benefit from.

In Hosea 4:6, the good book says that "My people are destroyed (suffer) for the lack of knowledge." Our predecessors shared their life experiences, gave us plenty of business tips, and rules to the game of life. All we have to do is duplicate their progressive steps to make them fit into our current day and time to be triumphant. History provides us a thousand answers for a thousand problems. Gaining knowledge is easy when it comes to reading. Applying that knowledge from what we've read is where the gold is hidden. "There's GOLD in dem thar books!"

"Books expand the mind and allow us to create new paths for ourselves. Using our imagination, and providing for others to use theirs, is an obligation for all."
PROFESSOR JEAN-CLAUDE EXULIEN

Tap into the mind of your favorite entrepreneur by reading their words in black and white. Written words are more than just letters beautifully put together. Letters represent symbols and images; both contain the limitless power to access our incredible subconscious mind. Reading unlocks the forces of the subconscious, which has been known to be a psychic activity just below the level of awareness. The beauty of it is that our subconscious mind registers images and symbols automatically without us even knowing it. Our brain sees words as pictures creating a visual dictionary that we tap into when it's time to utilize the information that the particular image represents. Our decisions, choices, and feelings are affected positively or negatively when a symbol or image has imprinted a certain idea into our mind. Feelings provoke thoughts. Thoughts provoke actions. Our actions create our reality; where and how we live, the quality of food that we eat, and whether we remain single or married are a few good examples. In other words, our behavior is impacted by what we see and read, and therefore our days ahead are also altered.

It's difficult to find time to sit down and study, correct? There are 7 days in a week, 4 weeks in a month, 30 days in a month, 12 months in a year, and 365 days in a year, unless it's the leap year and that gives us one extra day to be awesome! It takes 365 days, 5 hours, 48 minutes, and 47.5 seconds for the earth to make one complete lap around the sun. That means there is more than enough time for you to take the time to invest your money and time in a book that harmonizes with your life's purpose. Don't just read to get it out of the way. Take good notes, use a highlighter, and write small marks in the book if you have to — it's your book anyway. Review your notes once you're done reading for the day since there could be actionable items that you can start implementing to improve your life instantly. We are forever students of life learning something new every day.

"The backbone of success is hard work, determination, good planning, and perseverance."

MIA HAMM

One of the most valuable lessons you'll learn regarding planning for the future is that the more you plan ahead for anything, the better your chances of success will be. It can be for marriage, a new business plan, college career, marketing plan, a book or film script, or just life in general. You either plan for success or you plan to fail. Did you know that by writing your plans down, your chances of success automatically increase by 1000%? Yes, 1000%! Don't take my word for it, ask your local neuropsychologist to verify that statement.

According to neuroscience, vividly seeing our desire in written form is strongly associated with goal-setting and success. Setting goals have a direct link with higher self-esteem, motivation, self-confidence, and autonomy. Writing our goals down and visibly posting them either on our wall, journal, refrigerator, or even a sticky note on your computer, helps us remember them since sometimes we forget, especially when it comes to our long-term plans. It also allows us to act on them more frequently and easily seeing them since reminders are in your face. Writing our success goals down on paper starts a biological process called encoding, by which information travels to our brain's hippocampus (a part of the brain in charge of our ability to learn new things, motivation, emotion, and memory) where it's analyzed. Therefore, we remember what we've written down better than what we've simply read. To simplify the correlation, look at your success goals as you would the grocery list that you left behind on the refrigerator door on yourwwwwwwww way to the gym, but didn't realize it until you've reached the grocery store. You may not remember everything on your grocery list, but you can recall the main items written down. Now, when you combine the two processes, you've empowered yourself with a natural advantage and have increased your chances of overall success. [Feel free to hang up a positive message on your shower wall too.] It makes perfect sense.

Goal setting from a psychological perspective is an essential tool for self-motivation and drive, for both personal and professional levels. Having a goal gives meaning to our dreams, actions, and adds fuel to our faith, providing us with the jolt of energy to achieve something great. So, tell me, what is your excuse for not writing your goals down? Start now. Don't wait another second! I don't know about you, but I am not in the business of failing. Either you plan to succeed or you are planning to fail.

"Don't live with a can't do it attitude when you have a can-do power!"
JOEL OSTEEN

You'll notice people who have a losing attitude consistently make excuses. In fact, it's been scientifically proven that procrastination is often tied to those with low confidence, low self-esteem, or negative feelings about their ability to complete certain tasks. According to Dr. Judson Brewer, the director of research and innovation at Brown University's Mindfulness Center, our brains are always looking for relative rewards, and calls it the Bigger Better Offer. [6] Whenever we have

---

[6] Lieberman, Charlotte. Why You Procrastinate (It Has Nothing to Do With Self-Control). 2019, The New York Times

the habit of dancing around our tasks and haven't found a better reason to complete them, our brain is simply going to keep repeating the same thoughts until we give it something better to do. How do we fix this issue? We rewire our brain wires by forgiving our self for any past acts of procrastination.

The Achilles heel of many good people is procrastination, which is without a doubt a curse; it's an insidious disease that doesn't seem to be as bad as it really is to the individual suffering from it. Those with the disease are okay with being mediocre and just getting by. There is a misconception that it's a time management issue when it's really an emotion regulation problem. In other words, by significantly improving how we feel about ourselves, we'll automatically jump into completing the task at hand since we'll know the quality of our life will continue to increase and benefit based on our quick responses. Those who are susceptible to procrastination will give you a million excuses as to why they can't do this or that, but they'll find it hard to give you one reason why they can. Find your one reason. No one wants to live on Skid Row sleeping on broken dreams and glass bottles. Having a "can do" attitude makes a world of difference. It's all a part of your Winning Equation. How badly do you want to win?

Another key point to success is knowing the difference between being busy and being productive. Lord, have mercy! Please hear me out on what I am about to say. People get caught up in being busy but accomplish very little daily and are really chasing their tails. Then there are those who are successful busy bees but can't enjoy a lick of their success. You can be active without making progress. This is why having a task list for each goal is extremely helpful in not wasting valuable time. Life will literally pass us by if we don't take the time to enjoy the little moments that make the essence of our days on earth worth living.

You have to determine what success means to you before you can start your journey toward achieving it. Life will get shaky and mountains will grow out of nowhere to steer you away from your M.A.P. Defining our goals for success in the beginning also helps us maintain our vision of the expected result within our spirit and helps us to maintain our truth. In the game of chess, we call it the endgame. So, determine which is more important; the big house on the hill with a four-car garage or having a beautiful family in the home with you.

Perhaps, your goal is to become the president of a billion-dollar company, a top chef on the Food Network, or the leading scientist at MIT. Whatever it is, allocate time and energy to determining what that success truly looks like for you with as much detail as possible, then plan it out. You literally have to plan to win, plan for success, and plan for your life just as you would do for the construction of your new home, improving your credit score, or your children's education. It's entertaining to vicariously enjoy our favorite celebrities' riches and glory as we support their climb up the ladder of success. There is nothing like watching your favorite actor/actress, comedian, rapper, or singer doing what they do best on the big screen or on stage at a concert. Celebrate their success, however, INVEST IN YOURSELF too! I can't say it enough, INVEST IN YOURSELF!

Actually, you should invest more time and energy into accomplishing your dreams. You can't work on making your millions while watching three hours of football, basketball, or a tennis match. Those that you see on the big screen or on the stage at a concert are already financially set. That is why we must mind our business in order to live large and in charge too! And please don't forget to give reverence to the faithful few people in your corner. Loyal friends are hard to come by. Cherish them as if it's your last day on earth because you never know when either of you gots to go. Without them, you won't win. Many of the celebrities we put on high pedestals don't know us or even care about our well-being. For the most part, their goal is to please and manipulate the masses in order to keep raking in millions. Your aim is to distinguish yourself from the crowd; to be unique and authentic as you climb your way to the top while still maintaining a youthful spirit, staying in the right frame of mind, and while also continuing to help others along the way. Helping others shows your level of gratitude for the opportunities that have been divinely presented to you. One day they'll be helping someone else and so on and so forth.

Final Thoughts

Ask yourself: "What is it that I do best?"

Knowing what makes your heart pump harder with excitement, will be the key to get you over the hump. Find your one reason and don't hesitate to do what needs to be done.

Write down your dreams and give them a realistic lifeline completion date. A goal without a lifeline is a pipedream. We can't eat pies in the sky and be fulfilled. With great faith, due diligence, hard work ethics, and dedication, you'll achieve the success you've planned for. You must first write your dreams down on paper and write a clear plan so you will know what you need to breathe life into. Remember, you either plan for success or you plan to fail. Increase your chances of success by 1000%.

REVIEWING YOUR DREAMS: 5 IMPORTANT THINGS TO REMEMBER

- ⊃ Read your dreams with excitement. It's the positive feelings that get the blessings!
- ⊃ Imagine your goals unfolding in real-time.
- ⊃ Embrace your goals as you achieve them. Celebrate your wins. Learn from your losses.

- ⮞ Share your success with close friends/family. Your success is their success. Share the positive energy because they'll need the inspiration and support too for their own dreams.
- ⮞ Eradicate procrastination. Think about how great you'll feel once you've accomplished your goals. One step at a time.

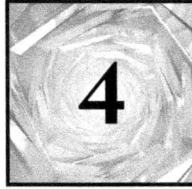

KEEP MOVING
FORWARD...
NO MATTER WHAT!

"**F**EAR" AND "TRYING" ARE TWO OF MY LEAST FA-vorite words in the world. "Fear" causes people to hesitate in moving forward, while "trying" mentally gives people a reason to jump ship before the boat even leaves the dock. Lions, tigers, sharks, Komodo dragons, and bears are all predatory animals to be fearful of. Their shear strength can rip flesh into shreds with just one swipe with their paws or juicy bite. On the yellow brick road of success, you're going to face plenty of predators of all sorts in your lifetime. They'll disguise themselves as friends, family, business partners, and co-workers while waiting for an opportune time to strike. You know exactly what I mean if you've worked in corporate America, especially at the executive level. Even when the inevitable happens, such as losing your job or a loved one, you must remain positive and keep moving forward with your dreams, no matter what.

Many of us want to quit or don't even start on our journey because of the fear that the support from our loved ones won't be there. When people tell you that they'll *try* to come to your special event or *try* to support you, it is a cop-out. This usually means they aren't coming, so don't hold your breath. Then you'll hear the "But, what happened was… blah blah blah." Over time, they'll sound like a broken record, however, please don't allow the discouragement to break your spirit. People make promises with good intentions all the time but rarely fulfill them. It takes a person of noble character to keep their word.

Many of us "but" their way right out of their blessings. "I could've won first place in the race, *but* I underestimated my competitors, and didn't practice enough." "The chicken soup would've been better, *but* I forgot to add the chicken." "I almost won a million dollars, *but* I forgot to play the numbers." Get rid of the buts. This is not the language or energy of winners. If you are that type of friend/family member that speaks with these words freely, take "try," and "but" out of your vocabulary since they're a part of a chicken's daily language; those words grant you an open invitation to give up at the slightest hint of a challenge without putting in a valiant effort. There will be times when you'll only be ten yards away from the finish line after running a full nine miles to get there. It would be absurd to give up at that point. Those last ten yards will take everything you've got in you. Physically, you won't have anything left, but spiritually, with the correct words of encouragement that you speak, you'll be able to tap into your abundance of supernatural powers to achieve the success goals you have in mind.

When we go into a situation with a *trying* mindset, we're making plenty of room to drown in doubts, and allow our fears to seep in instead of faith. Where there is faith, there is hope. Where there is hope, there is an opportunity for victory. Support your friends, family, and even perfect strangers given that you believe in their grind and vision; you're missing out on good fortune each time you bypass someone else's dream that was meant for you to plant a seed in. Don't try, just do it. By doing so, you become a source of strength. You'll also be feeding your own spirit with the nourishment it needs to reach your dreams. Not to mention, there will be times when you will need support from others as well. Support is a form of love that can come in the shape of attending their event, sharing their project through social media, email, and, especially, making a purchase—whatever it takes. Support gives trailblazers like you and I encouragement, and the reassurance to keep moving forward. In many cases, it allows us to overcome things, such as the fear of failure, rejection, and the Cookie Monster. All these fears sound familiar, right? Well, maybe not the last one, but on a serious note, some people walk around with fearfulness weighing heavily on their hearts and minds to the point of not being able to eat a single bit. Panic emits a level of negative energy that can ultimately create an avalanche of disappointment in our lives that prevents us from actualizing our expected outcome. We're in a dangerous place (state of mind) when our fears overpower our dreams. Thus, we successfully attract the opposite of our goals only to lock up our minds in a prison, and our spirit and body are bound to soon follow. We don't mean to, of course, but that's the end result.

One common and ancient principle is the Law of Attraction.[7] What you intensely think about is what you attract. What you meditate on, and then act and speak into the atmosphere is what you attract and manifest into your world.[8] There is a common misconception that everything will be peaches and cream if you only speak and think positively, or if you read nothing but edifying and spiritual books. That is not the case; I wish it were that simple. Manifesting your desires involves accepting that everything isn't in your hands to control, especially in team projects. However, many things are in your power to have sovereignty over. All you can do is your part in the spirit of excellence and surround yourself with supportive, positive people you can count on to do their part. I'm not talking about text buddies or online besties. I mean people in your real life who are genuinely excited for you that they actually pray for your

---

[7] Rhonda Byrne, "The Secret". Chicago, 2006, Simon & Schuster, Chicago, Page 53.

[8] Kevin Dorival, "7 Types of Queens, Kings Desires". Pompano Beach, Skyview Creative Circle, Page 309.

success and give you high fives before and after the victories. High fives are a great source of positive energy that electrifies everyone and promotes togetherness! They'll purchase your paintings, shop at your store, sit in your lectures, enjoy patronizing your salon, and dine at your restaurant. These types of supporters will take the extra steps to promote you to their circle of friends and associates with enthusiasm; they'll be honored to do so. In promoting you, they'll be promoting themselves too. That's the beauty about life—the energy is naturally reciprocated.

Sometimes it takes the support from others to help us see the winner within ourselves, especially while volunteering. If you are one of the unfortunate ones who didn't have loving parents, teachers, or mentors in your early stages of life to encourage you, it's even more important to have eagles around you today; they won't let you chicken out when things get difficult, instead, they'll lovingly challenge you to raise the bar. You must be positive and optimistic, even when the going gets tough. This is the time that the mentally tough keep on going!

An optimist rides the unpredictable waves of life and creates them too. On the other hand, the pessimist gets knocked down by the waves. You must learn to toss out the pessimistic, "could've, should've, would've" kinds of people from your dream flight if the plane headed towards your destiny plane is ever going to take off. If your dream only requires you to accomplish it, then your vision is too small. Teamwork literally makes the dream easier to accomplish. And if you faint at the sight of adversity, your faith is too weak. The perfect time to build up your faith muscles isn't while you're in the thick of things, but rather beforehand during peaceful times.

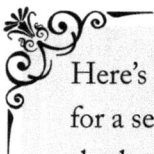

Here's a cliff note: Support those who support you. Don't think for a second it's a one-way street. Make it your business to wash the hands of those who wash yours; it's the right thing to do. One hand washes the other! Where you are going in life will

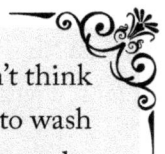

require an incredible amount of energy and focus, and a solid support base will help tremendously. Every army has allies, and you have to be a one-man army with real friends who will back you up. Many of us have fallen and are still falling into the trap of depending on social media followers that are here today and gone tomorrow. However insignificant that they may seem, online friends do have a role to play in expanding your brand and worldly presence. However, it isn't advised that you totally rely on them to increase your importance in our "new normal" society. It frightens some people not to get a lot of likes or a certain number of views on their videos. People take you more seriously with good old fashion networking at events; greeting people in person while looking at them in the eye with a firm handshake will always trump digital pleasantries.

As for me, my biggest fear in life wasn't death or speaking in front of a crowd. The fear of poverty had its ugly grip on me for as long as I can remember. Interestingly enough, that same fear was my biggest motivator to keep me moving forward regardless of how difficult it seemed. In the ghetto, where most of the residents are living just above or below the poverty line, there is a popular phrase that people say on a regular basis, unknowingly unbeknown to them that it's actually curse: "Ball til' you fall." It's catchy because it rhymes, and rappers use this cliché like it's a church hymn in their lyrics; many of them spoke their fall from greatness into existence. The mere thought of falling from the top of the success ladder should petrify anyone in their "right mind" to make the right decisions. Who wants to lose everything they fought and worked hard for? Whether it is a marriage or a family business that has been operating for years, anything worth having is worth fighting for.

Believe it or not, as tall, dark, and handsome as I am, my life was riddled with mistakes. Some were self-inflicted, and others came with the territory of being a trailblazer. Growing up in a single-mother household in the hood, you can almost say I inherited a few problems. We were bound to lose. There were times when we had to steal buckets of water from our neighbors to take a bath when our water was cut off; one five-gallon bucket and a plastic cup were enough for the four of us to properly cleanse ourselves. Things got so rough that we would sometimes laugh, on an empty stomach, to brighten up our spirits. Over time we learned to find the silver lining in the dark clouds of poverty and gun smoke. It's sad when tragedy becomes normal. Still, we just knew there had to be a life better than what we had. "Please, God, please!" was our battle cry.

As I matured, it was extremely hard to forgive myself for the scars that my heart, and body had to endure. I had to forgive my eyes for the ugliness they've seen. My siblings and peers witnessed one too many horrific ordeals that left us traumatized for years. We saw people get shot, stabbed, and killed before we knew how to write a full sentence. The 1982 classic hip-hop song "The Message" by Grandmaster Flash and the Furious Five has to be one of the most powerful songs ever written in entertainment history. It was truly a jungle, and I have no idea how we kept from going under. The favor of our Creator and our consistency towards bettering ourselves had to be what helped us persevere through it all.

The funny thing about going through those rough patches is that our smiles never went away. When overcoming challenges, it's better to go through them with a positive mindset and a smile. Each mountain we face represents a daunting task that is waiting for us to plant our victory flag on top of it. From this day forth, you will no longer tuck in your tail. You will march and you will overcome! Period.

Final Thoughts

Go through the fires and tornados of life with your head high, chest out, and dukes up! Smiling is your best asset and, many times it will be your only weapon. You should smile quite often. I can't stress enough how important it is to go through each battle with a joyful heart and the mindset that you already have the victory in your hands. Celebrate your wins and support your supporters. Take the phrases "but" and "I'll try" out of your vocabulary and make it happen!

5 Ways to Find a Reason to Smile

- In the morning, if you've been blessed to wake up—smile!
- Approach problems with the mindset that everything will work out in your favor.
- Motivate yourself by clapping yourself happy (if you're happy and you know it, clap your hands). It'll make you smile and feel great about yourself!
- Revisit a past victory in your mind. Replay it and smile at the same time.
- Fixate your eyes on flowers, birds, or anything that Mother Nature blessed the earth with.

PROTECT YOUR
POWER FLOW

*L*ET THERE BE LIGHT! YOUR BRAIN IS A BIG ELECTRO-
magnetic energy storage center that requires you to keep
the power on in order for it to operate efficiently and optimally. Being
optimistic and thankful requires enthusiastic energy; thinking about
what you are grateful for keeps your power flowing in a positive direction. Why? Gratitude helps us to see opportunities that the ungrateful
cannot envision. The more appreciative you are, the more bountiful your
blessings will be. For this reason, what you focus on with a high level
of energy will indeed manifest. Whatever you put the right energy and
focus towards will grow into a cornucopia of blessings flowing your way.
It's no coincidence that those with the stick-to-it-iveness attitude often
find themselves in a fortunate stroke of serendipity.

Write this down: *Where Attention Goes, Power Flows!* It takes
power to live, and without it we are lifeless. A battery with no power
is useless. Learn to control your attention. Get your mind right
by getting a hold of your thoughts. We've all heard of the saying,
"Collect Your Thoughts," and that's exactly what we must do when

we know that our thinking pattern is scattered making it impossible to obtain a peace of mind. Tell your mind what to think about by focusing on a specific topic. Friends, many of us keep getting paid with pain instead of reaping the financial rewards that reflects our hard work. We can't afford to not "mind our business" or pay attention to what we're consistently thinking about. One day your finances will match your efforts!

Brain Power Tip

Conscious parents with a solid financial background forbid their children from saying things, such as, "I can't afford it." Instead, they say, "*How* can I afford it?" The first phrase, "I can't", shuts down a person's brain-computer, and they no longer have to think. The second one puts the brain into action or overdrive, creating a conduit for possibilities, excitement, and dreams. It forces the brain to do what it does best: search for the answers to your questions and activate a new realm of imagination.

Consciousness governs experience. Experience cultivates wisdom. All the power and wealth in the world is worth nothing without the proper mindset to manage the resources. Everyone is the god of their own experience. You are not God over anyone else, so let's get that straight. There is only one almighty, all-knowing, omnipresent God. Every woman and man is a god of their own experience, and has the ability to follow their intuition which will lead them into making prosperous decisions rather than leading to calamity. In fact, the Kemetians (and many other African cultures) believed and saw themselves as gods having a human experience on Earth. We are always evolving to what we see ourselves being. People catch the flu or a cold during the winter because that is what the news media continues to pump into the public's minds. As a result, we pay attention to and attract the cold, and claim it even though it's usually just our allergies flaring up.

Where your attention goes, the power flows. When you aim your thoughts on the good aspects of your life, you create more of them—and sometimes even beyond your imagination. The mind is indeed a terrible thing to squander on negativity since doing so will only result in nightmarish outcomes. So, for this reason, you must endeavor to remove pessimistic people from your circle. Anyone that does not believe in you doesn't deserve to be around you. It does not matter if they are a family member or a friend. They could be an undercover hater or a flat-out foe, even if you refuse to acknowledge it. When you have a calling on your life, your glowing power will be obvious and will naturally attract people to you. Some of them will want to use you so that they can tap into your anointing for as long as they can, while others will simply desire to assist you along your journey. In due time, their true colors and intentions will be revealed. You don't have to worry about tomorrow's enemies when you have the authority to eliminate them today. There is no time like the present, so seize today as an opportunity to start evaluating your circle. History repeats itself; opportunities don't!

We often find ourselves asking for support, affirmation, and love, which are all fine things to wish from others; however, it is usually done in the wrong order. Besides, how many times have you asked for support and were disappointed by the lack thereof? Here's a bit of advice: First, start with supporting, affirming, and loving yourself! Give yourself the best shot at success by helping yourself before seeking external help. This way, you'll know exactly what you need. The fact remains that you have to believe in YOU, so don't ever stop—HOPING, DREAMING, and BELIEVING.

Now, I'm going to hold your hand as we time travel into the deep end of our planet's history to explain a difficult yet essential components of our lives. The Kemetians (original Ancient African civilization of Egypt around 20,000 BCE, possibly older) regarded the heart, rather than the brain, as the essential source of human wisdom and power. They knew the heart was connected to each individual's emotions, memories, manifestations, soul, and personality. When the human body was first mummified, they didn't put the brain into cognizance, and as such, it was pulled out through the nose with a special tool to be thrown away. Somehow, they understood that the heart was invaluable, and they were absolutely right! They understood that the heart communicated with the brain, emitting energy into our immediate environment, and aided in the creation of the world we live in. With that being said, what if I told you that your heart could think?

"Thought is a force—a manifestation of energy—
having a magnet-like power of attraction."
WILLIAM WALKER ATKINSON

Electricity is all around us—around the planet and even throughout the body, particularly in our brains. Our cells are equipped to conduct electrical currents, which enables the nervous system to send signals throughout the body and the brain, making it possible to move, think, articulate, and feel. On Earth, the flowing liquid metal in the planet's outer core generates electrical currents. The rotation of the Earth on its axis causes these electric currents to form a magnetic field extending around our planet. Why is this important? This magnetic field is critical to sustaining life on Earth. It protects us from high amounts of radiation from the Sun, and without it our atmosphere would leak into outer space.

The earth and the human race have a couple of things in common: Electricity plays a vital role in our survival. It's paramount to protect ourselves from both negative energy and unwanted radiation. As humans, we give off mostly infrared (thermal) radiation. Hi-tech toys like infrared cameras and binoculars allow us to see thermal radiation from other people and animals in the dark so you're be able to see them before they come close enough to attack. I say all of that for this reason, we must do what we can to avoid people with foul intentions and hateful (negative) energy without the use of special cameras. This is where our spiritual discernment comes in to evaluate those around us.

But let us get back to the heart of the matter. There's a misconception in today's world that people are smarter now than they were in ancient times but get this: The heart's electrical field is about sixty to one hundred times greater in amplitude than the electrical activity generated by our brain-computer, which contains an estimated eighty billion brain cells. The Kemetians didn't have an electrocardiogram (ECG) to measure the heart's electrical signals as we know it — or maybe they did; how did they know this science, which was invited in 1887 thousands of years before modern-day technology? Your guess is as good as mine. So, who's smarter? One thing is definite, they were highly intelligent people and had a fully functioning society running on all cylinders without the use of the internet or hi-speed computers.

According to the HeartMath Institute, the magnetic field produced by the heart is more than five thousand times greater in strength than the field generated by the brain. It can even be detected about three feet away from the body, 360 degrees around you.[9] It looks as if it's really the heart that is the most terrible thing to waste. Our brains are magnetic and will glue onto whatever it is willingly or unwillingly exposed to. This is why one must intentionally read positive books, have intellectually engaging conversations, and attend positive meetings/events on a daily basis to fight off the negativities we're exposed to.

Furthermore, the supercomputer known as our brain is made to

---

[9] McCraty, Dr. Rollin., "The Science of Heart Math: The Heart-Brain Connection," https://www. heartmath.com/science/

analyze, answer questions, and absorb information through our five gates (senses): sight (eyes are the "window to the soul"), touch (hands/feet), hearing (ears), smell (nose), and taste (mouth). It's wise to control what you're being conditioned to do by guarding your five gates. With that being said, when our brain trinity (mind, heart, and gut) are working together, anything can happen. Anything! I bet you didn't know you had a trio of brains. At the maximum level, the ideal situation is that the three brains are working in synchrony, with billions of neurons cooperating to produce a harmonic sound like a symphony, harnessing a constantly modifying network of neurons that work in sync to accomplish your worthwhile desires.

THE ROLE OF THE THREE BRAINS

Although the brains of the head, heart, and gut work together, they have different physical functions. When you're able to align all three, you're able to avoid internal conflicts, or "cognitive dissonance" as it's called in psychology. The trio's alignment eliminates doubt, which is the cardinal sin when believing in oneself. Cognitive dissonance is characterized by having beliefs, ideas, or behaviors that contradict each other.[10] Who hasn't experienced this? We all have to some degree. These internal conflicts become prevalent when we're faced with opposing demands, important business plans, and moral decisions; they slow down our ability to make power moves in the right direction, therefore, we must reduce the contradictions as much as possible. You can't lose battles both internally and externally and expect to win the war. Securing your home base first (mind, body, and spirit) gives us peace in every sense of the word. It's also the best way to prepare yourself for the battles ahead.

Your *brain trinity* performs different mental and emotional roles that shape your physical and spiritual world, as mentioned throughout this book.

---

[10] Saul McLeod, "Cognitive Dissonance," February 5, 2018. https://www.simplypsychology.org/cognitive-dissonance.html.

- The **Head-Brain** analyzes information and applies logic.
- The **Heart-Brain** senses the world through emotion, wisdom, and feelings.[11] the heart-brain has about forty thousand neurons that can sense, feel, learn, and remember. The heart is not just a pump; it has its neural network or "little brain."
- The **Gut-Brain** is also directly connected to your head brain by a newly discovered neuron circuit. The human gut is connected by more than one hundred million nerve cells. This makes it a brain itself, which means it has its own nervous system.

"For as a man thinketh in his heart, so is he."
PROVERBS 23:7

Change your thoughts, and you'll change your words. Change your words, and you will change the world! "As a man, thinketh" scripture leads me to believe that they understood that the heart has the capacity to think independently from the brain. What we're thinking in our head is often different from what we're thinking deep down inside our gut and in our hearts. As long as you think you can do or become something then you probably can. Whatever you think you can't do or become, then you're right on that too. Motivation deals with what's in our heads. Its job is to get us to take action, to get up and do something before it's too late. You are so much stronger than you think. Inspiration deals with our hearts and spirit. Our brain may think something is logically impossible while the heart is all in, ignoring the brain's logic all together telling us to go after "what we feel" is the right move. Top athletes have been known to dedicate a game to a fallen loved one and go beyond their normal talents performing with record-breaking performances. Everything you think you can feel and

---

[11] Alshami, Ali M. "Pain: Is It All in the Brain or the Heart?" November 4, 2019. Pub Med.Gov https://pubmed.ncbi.nlm.nih.gov/31728781/

therefore you're able to put your thoughts into physical actions that can manifest into something tangible. For this reason, it also pays huge dividends to often eat as healthily as possible because our brain's trinity level of functionality is based on our diet. We are not only what we thinketh, but we are also what we eat.

A healthy gut contributes to a happy life by impacting whether you have a strong or weak immune system to fight off diseases and common infections. Eating the right foods, such as citrus fruits, red bell peppers, broccoli, garlic, ginger, spinach, and almonds fortifies you and your family's immune system. Also, a healthy sleeping patterns help us avoid being grouchy, and promote a properly functioning heart and brain, which is utterly important for clearer thinking. If that's not enough, to prove to you how vital the gut is, it also improves our mood, length of peaceful sleep (better dreams), and digestion; it may even help prevent some cancers and autoimmune diseases. However, a clean gut doesn't equate to courage. Here's a story about a young boy who rose up the army ranks from the ground up with more guts than a hundred men. His self-motivation led him to envision that one day he'd build an incredible structure on top of a mountain in the Caribbean paradise, originally known as Saint Domingue, the French colony island of Hispaniola. It was once known as the richest colony in the world, due to its mass production of sugar and coffee.

Additionally, the small island was among the global leaders in indigo, cacao, and cotton with 8000 plantations producing 40% of the world's sugar and 60% of the coffee exported to Europe. With the luxury of forced labor that slavery provided, the French slave masters was able to annually ship 150–170 million *livres* worth of goods back home to France. That's the equivalent of $981,025,925 in today's dollars.[12] The United States of America and all European countries were built on the backs of enslaved Africans. It's truly unfortunate that both

---

[12] James, CLR. "The Black Jacobins: Toussaint L'Ouverture and the San Domingo Revolution." (New York, Random House) 1989.

governments refuse to pay any kind reparations; even though the descendants around the world continues to suffer from the repercussions of slavery in the 21st century, nearly five hundred years later. Only time will tell if and when justice will ever be served.

Unbeknownst to most people, on October 9, 1779, 545 free Haitian soldiers volunteered on behalf of the French army to journey to Savannah, the oldest city in Georgia. The soldiers came to fight against the British army during the American Revolutionary War. They were called The Chasseurs-Volontaires de Saint-Domingue.[13] One of the soldiers was a twelve-year-old, brave drummer boy named Henri Christophe, who would later become the self-proclaimed king of Haiti, changing his name from Henri to King Henry Christophe. He formed the first and only monarchy in Haiti's history. On top of that, he built the world-famous Citadelle Laferrière, a beautiful fortress with a total of sixty-five cannons pointing out of the windows. It took thirteen years to build this edifice on top of a mountain three thousand feet in the sky, and it is only accessible by horse, mule, or a long two-hour seven-mile uphill hike (completed in 1820). The UNESCO (United Nations Educational, Scientific, and Cultural Organization) designated the Citadelle as a World Heritage Site in 1982. It is also considered one of the Seven Wonders of the World by history scholars, and is the largest fortress in the Western Hemisphere as it serves as a symbol of Haitian independence and strength.

Living up to his title, King Henry didn't disappoint, as he also built one of the most marvelous palaces in the world in 1813 called Sans-Souci (its French for "carefree" or "no worries"), which is located only three miles from the Citadelle in the city of Milot, the northern part of the island. It leads me to believe that the area was the king's favorite location from a military strategic standpoint, and after seeing the

---

[13] George P. Clark *Phylon*, The Role of the Haitian Volunteers at Savannah in 1779: An Attempt at an Objective View. Vol. 41, No. 4 (4th Qtr., 1980), pp. 356-366

beautiful landscape anyone could understand why. There are thousands of lush trees and bright flowers surrounding the Citadelle making the natural energy intoxicating. There's a constant cool breeze just over the hills coming from the Atlantic Ocean, which is visible from the roof of the historic building. The area is majestic with hundreds of birds flying through the clear sky complimenting the breathtaking view and the cool crisp fresh air.

After years of studying Haitian history, I finally visited the land of my ancestors in 2016 to personally witness these two marvelous structures. It was a blessing to finally enjoy the rich culture that I read so much about. Those who have seen it can testify that these buildings are just as magnificent as they're described here. Everyone should visit and support their homeland's tourist economy. The locals depend on the new money being brought to their community.

Nevertheless, before Henri Christophe changed his name to King Henry, he was a lieutenant for several years. Henri served under the leadership of the greatest military strategist of the 18th and 19th century, and possibly of all time, General François-Dominique Toussaint L'Ouverture, who was knighted and recognized as an extraordinary military warrior, and brilliant statesman. There's a known conspiracy to downplay the general's unforgettable achievements due to the superpowers he defeated in war, fair and square, and the color of his skin. For this reason, it's my honor and duty to present to you the real-life super hero that saved hundreds of thousands of lives, and simultaneously inspired millions of revolutionary soldiers and thinkers around the globe. He coined the phrase, "Slavery anywhere is slavery everywhere," before achieving an incredible victory against France's Napoleon Bonaparte Army, the greatest military power of that time, at the height of its power, during the Haitian Revolution.[14]

The war lasted from 1791 to 1803 and continues to echo in

---

[14] Jean-Bertrand Aristide, "Toussaint L'Ouverture: The Haitian Revolution" (Verso Books: 17 Oct 2008)

classrooms of scholars and street corners today. General Toussaint added L'Ouventure to his name, which means "Opening," "One Who Finds the Way," and "The Enlightened One." It's my opinion the name change boasted his spiritual powers, along with his confidence in the political arena and battlefields. Together with a couple of other brave revolutionary freedom fighters, such as Makandal, Dutty Boukman (pronounced Book-man, meaning "man of the book"), Jean-Jacques Dessalines, Marie Roze Adam, and Alexandre Sabès Pétion—they shook the world! The 500,000 Haitian men and women of the island were completely against their enslavement and fought to regain their freedom. On January 1st, 1804, Jean-Jacques Dessalines took over after the capture of their leader, and claimed the island's independence making it the first country to permanently abolish the institution of slavery. To win this war was a real-life Mission Impossible made possible by everyone involved having faith, courage, self-respect, self-motivation, self-discipline, and the meeting of the minds for their freedom.

Their mindset took an incredible amount of self-worth, spiritual power, vision, willpower, faith, and confidence to leave the gigantic mark in the history books that dare to tell the truth. This war single-handedly changed the course of history and the world's view on slavery. The rapacious slave owners convinced themselves through propaganda and evil intentions that people of African lineage loved to be bound. This was done in order to continue the most inhumane enterprise in world history since they were profiting enormously from it. Due to the auspicious acts of brave souls from Haiti's small island, an untold number of rebellions for freedom were sparked worldwide. This was the epitome of what we call a game-changer. Quite frankly, if there is a history class — more specifically, a Black history—course, book, or program that the Haitian Revolution isn't featured in, then it's a white-washed, watered-down version of history.[15]

---

[15] Dorival, Kevin, "Real Super Hero's: Haiti's Chassuier Volunteer De Saint Dominique At The Battle Of Savannah Part 1," November 30, 2019. https://kevindorival.com/real-super-heros-haitis-chassuier-voluntter-de-saint-dominique-at-the-battle-of-savannah-part-1/

This is how significant the Haitian Revolution impacted civilization in the late eighteenth and early nineteenth centuries. It was and still is, one of the best examples of a group of people with the correct self-perception, self-respect, and vision for their future. It's clear that the universe was with them because they bossed up and collectively defeated Goliath. Some enemies are simply too big to take on by yourself. The physical and mental shackles weren't a part of their plan. They knew better than anyone that slavery is catastrophic to the human spirit. And once you've lost your spirit the will to live will be no longer exist. This revolution was the catalyst to eradicate the mind control that their oppressors had over their thoughts and actions. A thinking person can never be a slave. Whenever you don't have control of your thoughts and body, someone else will. In 1933, Carter G. Woodson's groundbreaking book, The Mis-Education of the Negro, discusses the ramifications of allowing others to control you with ill intentions.

"If you can control a man's thinking you do not have to worry about his action. When you determine what a man shall think you do not have to concern yourself about what he will do. If you make a man feel that he is inferior, you do not have to compel him to accept an inferior status, for he will seek it himself. If you make a man think that he is justly an outcast, you do not have to order him to the back door. He will go without being told; and if there is no back door, his very nature will demand one."

Acknowledging who your enemies are enables you to channel your faith and energy toward defeating them and breaking their stronghold on you, if there is one. For it is written that we should be as gentle as a dove yet wise as a serpent. King Henry Christophe saw himself as someone important before it physically manifested to the world, and so should you. Never allow anyone to determine your value and self-worth. This is ultimately up to you to figure out.

HOW TO SET UP A WINNING PSYCHOLOGICAL FOUNDATION

#1. Higher Value System

Everyone should have some sort of value system. Having positive values allows us to have boundaries, which prevents us from being all over the place, doing whatever with whomever, whenever, and potentially placing ourselves and our loved ones' very lives in danger. Let's keep in mind your values are an internal matter that has nothing to do with material wealth or the name brands that you're devoted to. Having values means you've set your self-worth high, know what you stand for, and what you'll fight against. Those with a high-value system typically exhibit the following characteristics:

- Kindness
- Self-Responsibility
- Self-Discipline
- Self-Sufficiency
- Self-Direction
- Self-Awareness
- Self-Worth

#2. Recognize Your Mental Qualities

Acknowledge that the good attributes of your mind exist. It's okay to give yourself some credit. Recognize them as often as possible. By doing so will energize your mind to dig deeper into the subconscious for those breakthrough money-making ideas and witty inventions that you've been waiting for. In other words, anything that is recognized is energized. You can direct your power to flow toward your imagination, ideas, and positive desires. You'll be calling the qualities and attributes of your mind into action. Appreciate the different aspects of your existence and powers of being. Your presence is a present. You are a gift, and don't you forget it! You have the God-given power to make a positive difference in the world. Ignore the fact that you may not currently be in the best financial position or maybe seeking government assistance; it doesn't make you any less of person. You are still awesome if you choose to be. Having class has nothing to do with your finances. Welfare has its place, but don't make it your resting place!

#3. Discipline Your Brain

Do not allow your mind to wander or dwell on negative things; it's too easy to go off the deep end with that type of thinking patterns. Our imagination can work as a blessing or a hex, so you must be careful to "mind your own business." Your business is your gold mind; your gold mind is your business. Place your mind and actions on positive vibrations (volunteering, working on future projects, love, etc.) as much as possible. The moment you begin to dwell on something painful, whether it's about yourself or someone else, quickly snap out of it. Remind yourself that you are better than the poison that is trying to consume your mind and then control you. Think of the ramifications if you act out your stinking thinking. Replace those foul thoughts with your favorite memories, for instance, your best athletic plays, musical performance, or academic achievements. Perhaps it's a favorite activity that brought you great joy — a good calm spot on the beach, a place where you love to worship, or your favorite book. The discipline of the mind is fundamentally one of the most important components of your life. Self-control itself is a significant indicator of an individual's future success, whether it be the prediction of good health with little to no sickness, accumulating wealth, better relationships, and no criminal behavior. Sounds like a good life.

Final Thoughts

Having mental boundaries will save you tons of time and money. Look at excessive gamblers in a casino. The more cash they lose, the more absurd they become in losing, even more, thinking that they're going to hit it big. To put it another way, if your mind isn't right, nothing else will matter because it's the captain of your ship, the motherboard of your supercomputer.

It's paramount that your mind functions are disciplined, which will take some practice. Limit cognitive dissonances as much as possible, since having a peace of mind depends on it. If not, your billions of brain cells will act like an unruly pack of dogs, fighting and chasing their tails, and creating havoc in the form of brain cavities that block your problem-solving and creative capabilities. It will leave mildew behind instead of successful ideas. Your power will flow in the right direction based on the strength of the mental foundation that you've created.

7 WAYS TO GET YOUR POWER FLOWING IN THE RIGHT DIRECTION

- ⮑ Start with firmly supporting, affirming, and loving yourself.
- ⮑ Positive and optimistic thinking helps you see opportunity when times are tough. And they will get tougher so get ready. You'll be more than okay.
- ⮑ Gratitude helps you see openings where the ungrateful can't. All they can see are doors being closed.
- ⮑ Allow your supercomputer (brain) to work for you by asking, "How can I make this happen?" Stop automatically saying, "I can't or "this is impossible," when faced with a daunting task. Overwhelming situations are part of life, it brings the winner within you out.
- ⮑ Where attention goes, power flows. When your thoughts and feelings are aimed on the good aspects of your life, you create more of them. That's a great thing!
- ⮑ Allow your Brain Trinity to work in harmony as your personal symphony creating, your positive vibrations you live and thrive in.
- ⮑ A thinking person can never be a slave.

6

MENTAL MAKEOVER: REPROGRAMMING YOUR BRAIN

*T*HE BRAIN INSIDE OF THE HUMAN SKULL IS A COMplex system of networks that form trillions of neural patterns, continually looking for new neural paths or connections. It can only obtain these new neural paths when we are learning, thinking, and asking questions. With all of this electromagnetic activity going on upstairs, we can find ourselves with brain gaps that simply need a mental floss. Now, if the holes are deep and old, it may be time for a Mental Makeover, a renewal of the mind. So, the question is, how do you know that you need to reprogram your mind?

Now, presuming that your divine mind is filled with stinking thinking, like constant sexual activities, violence, thievery, or if your first response to everything is "no" and "can't-do-it" (negative demeanor), then it's time to consider a Mental Makeover. I know this because those were my thoughts, and they never helped me get anywhere I wanted to be. In fact, I, like many of us, dug myself into the abyss of doubt that seemed impossible to get out of. I simply took a deep look at my position in life by being real with myself about how I got in those chaotic situations. I kept telling myself, "This is not how my story will end!" And I was able to write a desirable future instead of an apathic one.

The next reasonable step was to swallow my pride and seek advice from my mentors on how to get out of that situation and to guide me on the steps to make better decisions. Once I got out—I did my best to stay out! My intentions were right. My plan was right. Therefore, my actions were correct. The only way to accomplish the daunting task of pulling myself out of the quicksand and back into a balanced life where I had control of it was to recalibrate my mind, body, and spirit.

"I prayed for twenty years but received no answer until I prayed with my legs."
FREDERICK DOUGLASS

You can pray, sing, and read, and watch all the inspirational programs on television, or march and protest until you're blue in the face. Fredrick Douglass, the prolific writer and orator of the 19th century, taught us an invaluable lesson regarding praying and action—nothing will change until you get your mind right and start praying with your legs. You cannot become successful by thinking about whether you're going to be successful or not. You become successful by consistently doing something with what you've been blessed with to make yourself a success. Or you can continue chasing pipe dreams year after year, expecting something different each new year, while continuing to do nothing about achieving what you're passionate about which is insanity and absurd. While we're on the subject, mental illness is a brain malfunction, but society keeps charging it as a character deficiency.[16]

This doesn't mean that people who are experiencing mental illness are instantly bad folks at all, but rather, their mind has broken down

---

[16] True Word Of Yeshua. (2020, June 14) Pastor Bryant, Jamal. "I Feel Like I'm Losing It." YouTube video, 5:55. https://youtu.be/_zsChk9dpY0

and is bombarded with an immense amount of pressure. It's essential that your mind is on point so that you are capable of dealing with the thousands of thoughts that run through it daily. Your thoughts are similar to our feelings, if you don't control your thoughts, they'll absolutely control you. Both are too powerful not to be tamed so that you can focus your resources.

Did you know that in 2005, the National Science Foundation published a fascinating article summarizing the research on daily human thoughts?[17] The conclusion of the research was fascinating! The average person has about 12,000 to 60,000 thoughts per day. Of those thousands of thoughts, 80% were negative, and 95% were the same repetitive thoughts from the day before. It's a daily internal struggle, a tug of war between good and evil, which gives room to cognitive dissonances that were mentioned in the previous chapter. We don't have a little demon or guardian angel sitting on our shoulders, but you better believe that we do have them guiding us in our minds. The good news is that 85% of what we worry about will never happen, and 97% of our worries are without merit and are planted in our minds from unfounded pessimistic perceptions. Negative thoughts are like having a few roaches in your kitchen, if proactive actions aren't taken on a consistent basis, it's guaranteed that you'll have an infestation of them on your mind.

We can run from many challenges and obstacles, but the one battle we can't hide, run, or take a vacation from is our mind. It's a constant battle for most, and just a temporary phase for others to whom will be in control. This is a mind science, which means that there's proven steps to secure the manifestation of your good thoughts and feelings. We can easily win by taking the time out to practice breathing techniques, while meditation and decide we'll be as positive as possible, as frequently

---

[17] Antanaitye, Neringa. "Mind Matters: How To Effortlessly Have More Positive Thoughts." https://tlexinstitute.com/how-to-effortlessly-have-more-positive-thoughts/

as possible. Nobody is happy-go-lucky every single day of their lives. If you can conjure up to feel the feeling of good health, wealth, and peace in your mind, that feeling will get the blessing. One must strive to maintain a positive state of mind, inner centeredness, mindfulness, and mental strength. Direct those billions of beautiful brain cells toward your dreams, and you'll reach the success you've been consistently striving for. Remind yourself: it's only a matter of time.

All bank accounts and human brains aren't created equal since both require adding something in order for them to grow. According to the University of Chicago School of Medicine, scientists estimate that the average human brain contains nearly a "hundred billion neurons" and the popular, but mistaken notion, that we use only 10% of our brain. We all accepted it, without question, just like many of the false history and religious dogmas we've been taught. For decades, top experts and professors have accepted this, until 2005, when the well-respected Brazilian neuroscientist Dr. Suzana Herculano-Houzel, impressively discovered a cutting-edge way to count the neurons in the brain of different species. Dr. Houzel concluded that humans have an average of eighty-six billion brain cells (perhaps a few billion extra, but who's counting).[18] A neuron is the basic unit of the brain cell, a complex network system that forms trillions of interconnected neural patterns.[19] Each of those neurons makes tens of thousands of contacts with other cells, bringing the number of neural connections into the quadrillions, or a million billion.[20]

Think of your brain cells as gigabits (GB) of memory space on your smartphone or high-powered supercomputer. It will store and project whatever you command it to do. If you want to pull up a website or

---

[18] Dr. Herculano-Houzel, Suzana, "The Human Brain In Numbers: A Linearly Scaled-Up Primate Brain, November 9, 2009. Frontiers in Human Neuroscience. https://www.frontiersin.org/articles/10.3389/neuro.09.031.2009/full#B28

[19] Mitchum, Rob, "Neuroscientist Leads Unprecedented Research To Map Billions Of Brain Cells," May 31, 2018. University of Chicago Neuroscientist leads unprecedented research to map billions of brain cells - UChicago Medicine

[20] Mitchum, Rob, "A Journey To Map The Mind," June 25, 2018. University of Chicago https://www.uchicago.edu/features/a_journey_to_map_the_mind/

research a topic, you simply type it in the search bar. These days, you can verbally tell your phone what to look up, then it will automatically speak and display a plethora of options per your request. The same applies to your brain. Instead of filling your supercomputer with negativity, the usual curse words, defeat, failure, violence, and poverty, replace them with words of affirmation, victory, love, generational wealth, family, and increase in every blessed way possible. This is easier to do when you genuinely love yourself and honor others, and that love and honor will be given unto you. It's a terrible thing not to utilize the untapped resources of your brain's power. The truth of the matter is a lot of us just weren't taught the dynamics of our mind outside of catchy rhetoric, "use your head to get rich", "work smarter, not harder", or "think big!"

However, to think big, you have to be around people and read books by those who were able to. According to my family and their beliefs, becoming wealthy was and still is an indication of being greedy, evil, and on the road to Hell. Generally speaking, this was, and still is, to a degree, the mindset of my community, the black community. It wasn't until I started surrounding myself with successful entrepreneurs that I began to think bigger and fly higher through the storms instead of just running my mouth while comfortably flapping my wings in a golden cage. I love listening to goal-getters and trailblazers who want more out of life and are consistently pursuing their dreams. [Notice I used the word *pursuing* and not chasing.] When you're "chasing" your dreams and the things you want out of life, you will become weary, tired, and may quit on your ambitions causing you to becalmed. Ambition without knowledge is a gorgeous yacht on a dry desert. In order for your dreams to come true sometimes takes hanging on to the ropes on the side of the ship in a storm with everything you got — just don't let go or jump ship. That's the bottom-line. There are so many dreams that sunk to the bottom of the ocean because the dreamer gave up or passed away. "Pursuing" means you're passionately going after your heart's goals for as long as you have to. When you're physically too tired to continue, your fiery spirit will push you beyond your mental and physical limits. It's inevitable that you'll be victorious!

Over the years, I've enjoyed working with extraordinary individuals who wrote down their future plans and maximized their mind power to their fullest potential. One such person is the sharp and wealthy civil attorney Willie Gary, Esq., The Giant Killer, who has a net worth of over $15 million as of 2021. He owns two fancy private jets and ten Bentleys. One of those jet planes is a stealthy black beauty with gold pinstripes. Imagine walking into your private jet with matching pinstripes. Wow! I knew I'd someday meet him after reading a *Black Enterprise* magazine article that featured the all-star attorney while I was in a jailcell. Praying and actively working on achieving that goal pulled the dream of working with him into reality. At the same time, I was thinking about how hanging around chickens landed me in the county jail for a year; how did I allow myself to be peer pressured into such a foolish decision? Easy. Birds of a feather will get either locked up or will boss up together. It wasn't a coincidence that I read about him at that particular time and space when I was a lost soul in a dark place. Just like Joseph's story in the Bible, I didn't focus on my current situation as my final destination. Knowing that there was so much more life in me gave me the self-motivation to move towards my goals and not dwell on my mistakes.

Four years later, in 2007, I was invited, through my mentor Ms. Marie Brown, to the world-renowned 15th Annual Willie Gary Foundation Kids Carnival, aka the Christmas Block Party. Some people can buy the bar and pay for everyone to enter a club for about $10,000. Mr. Gary bought downtown every year for fifteen years straight! He rented the entire beach and provided his guests free everything — food, wine, video games, and rides for the children — at a price tag of $2 million. The entrance fee was expensive: two canned goods. It was a fantastic event with top of the line catered foods and several celebrities in attendance: Don King, Biz Markie, Patti Labelle, former U.S. President Bill Clinton, and the cherry on top was that we got to see one of my favorite bands performing LIVE, The O' Jays! You're probably wondering how did I get to work with him, right?

One of the board members from the community group I volunteered with for several years, The Dr. Martin Luther King, Jr. Celebration Committee, just so happened to be best friends with his secretary's assistant. Once I realized that I knew two people who had direct contact with Mr. Gary, it was only a matter of time, space, and a written plan to connect with him. In my mind, all I had to do was create an opportunity instead of waiting on one to arise. At the time, I was in the preproduction stage for my first film and documentary, *The Courage to Believe: Never Give Up*, which encourages students not to give up on their dreams or give in to peer pressure. *Viola!* I pitched my idea to his secretary, and she loved it. Mr. Gary just so happens to have invested tons of time and money into helping urban youth get to and through college with his foundation. Fast forward, a scheduled interview was set for months later but was moved up once another one of his meetings was canceled. The day after I got the call, I called in sick from work, and my camera guy and co-producer, Ephraim Cambronne, was more than willing to join me for the road trip.

Off the record, Mr. Gary shared with me how he purchased the same hotel he once worked at as a teenage busboy and turned it into his headquarters, just like he imagined it. Equally impressive, his secretary also had a secretary, and his grandiose office was on the entire second floor overlooking the Atlantic Coast. Despite being a child of sharecroppers, having to sometimes walk to school barefoot, and of short stature, he focused on being great one day. He knew that life had so much more instore and nothing was going to steer him away from his dream. And rightfully so, he took it upon himself to promote himself from being a migrant worker to becoming one of the best personal injury lawyers in U.S. history.

In 2014, he won a $24,000,000,000 in a wrongful death case against

R.J. Reynolds Tobacco Company (the manufacturer of Pall Mall and Camel cigarettes) for misleading the public and government as to the dangers of smoking; I studied this subject and the hierarchy of the U.S. government extensively in college due to my political science major. During our documentary interview, he blessed me with advice on how to win in life, "Work hard, and don't be afraid to burn the midnight oil." Sitting there listening to him was a dream come true. I realized that there were so many dreams stuck within me; I decided that I couldn't sit still as they faded away deep into the ocean. Like Mr. Gary, I wanted so much more out of life and was determined to work hard to achieve everything I set my mind to!

Less than a month later, guess who I bumped into again at a youth conference in Jacksonville, Florida? I almost couldn't believe it! We were both guest speakers for different sessions. We cracked a couple of jokes together, and he blessed me again with one of the most profound compliments of my young career: "You got a great heart, Mr. Dorival. Keep doing what you're doing for our youth. I think it's great, your film will take you places! Don't you ever give up young man! If I can help—you know how to reach me."

Brain Facts

The adult human brain is comprised of 75 percent water, weighing an average of 1.4 kilograms (three pounds), and houses about eighty-six to one hundred billion neurons. That comes to about seventy million neurons per gram or thirty-three billion per pound. We lose about seventy million neurons a year, which equates to about 190,000 per day. Yikes! To build more neurons, you can do a few things, like eat blueberries and dark chocolate, keep your mind engaged with strategy games like chess, exercise regularly, and drink green tea.

When the brain is functioning on a full tank of water, you'll be able to think faster, be more focused, and experience greater clarity. A bonus to your winning equation is that you're enabling yourself to tap into a higher level of creativity and problem-solving skills. Water is also vital for delivering nutrients to the brain trio, along with other parts of our body and is needed to remove toxins. When the brain is fully hydrated, the exchange of nutrients and toxins will be more efficient — thus ensuring better concentration and mental alertness. Drink a glass of room temperature water when you wake up; do the same before you start counting the sheep.

How much water you should drink daily depends on a few variables, such as weight, activity, gender, and height. Dehydration causes your brain to run slower than usual, definitely not at its full RPM speed. Some of the mental symptoms of dehydration include brain fog, afternoon fatigue, focus issues, depression, anger, exhaustion, headaches, sleep issues, stress, and a lack of mental clarity and acuity. Instead of picking up coffee or soda to keep you up, try drinking a bottle or cup of water.[21] By the way, your body is about 70% water and 30% blood. Our lungs are comprised of 83 % water, skin stands at 64%, and muscles are in the mid 70's percentile. Drink more water because your body and mind will love you for it.

Another great, spiritually rich, and wealthy person I know is my pastor from back home, Bishop Edward Brinson. Between him and his wife, Yvette "Momma" Brinson, they own several real estate properties and churches all over Florida, New York, and the Caribbean islands. They both have super high ambitions, spiritually and financially. Some

[21] "Your Brain on H2O." University of California, Davis. 2, December 2015, https://shcs.ucdavis.edu/blog/archive/healthy-habits/your-brain-h2o

people have a problem with spiritual leaders earning a lot of money, but I certainly don't see it from that perspective. If you used your mindpower and sweat equity to put in the necessary hard work to manifest your dreams, you deserve all the bells and whistles that comes with the territory in my book. They taught me many great things, especially how to fly higher above whatever situation mentally and spiritually I found myself in. Pastor Ed often uses eagles' as analogy during his sermons, which rubbed off and caused me to utilize it too. Flying higher allowed me to see a life outside of my family's lack that I was accustomed to; it gave me the vision to distinguish between those that were doing their best to lift others up, those that love just hanging around, and those that somehow find joy tearing others down. Listening to his stories, whether it was from the pulpit, TBN (Trinity Broadcasting Network), or a private conversation, you'll be convinced that he could've been an NFL football star, CEO of a Fortune 500 company, or a Drug Kingpin. However, Pastor Ed, followed his spirit, love for his wife, and became an evangelist, a father, and then a pastor. A pretty darn good one too!

Eventually, I began looking in the mirror and saying to myself, "I should want better! I deserve better! I am more than a conqueror!" By constantly speaking those words of victory, I began to believe it was possible. As my self-perception improved, my confidence elevated as well. If, when reading these words, you don't feel that way about yourself, you will, after reading a few more pages from this book. We are going to do some intentional rewiring of your brain that will empower you to think bigger, a lot bigger. Many of us think too small and don't even realize it due to our condition. The sad part is the fact that no one around us is reaching higher. Your success can be the key that unlocks the blessings for many people that you love, and those who look up to you. The best part is that you'll enhance the lives of perfect strangers because you simply stepped into your purpose, fully engaged. It's unfortunate how many families are destroyed because someone refused to accept their calling in life? You're truly blessed when you can prevent a tragedy from happening in someone else's life.

It's my desire that your cup overflows with favor. Some people feel the rain, while the rest just get wet. May God continue to rain blessings all over you that there won't have enough room to store them. The amazing part of it all is that you won't get a chance to meet all the folks you've been a blessing to. Your cup will overflow so much with the favor that your friend's friends and your children's classmates will benefit simply through their association with you. Your children's children will go to college and start their own businesses helping them escape the clutches of a hard life by reaping from the financial rewards you have gained. For many years, Momma Brinson saw herself as a "Distribution Center." She happily gave away cars, clothes, and money to people who were in need or when she just wanted to be a blessing. She would often boldly tell us, "If God can get the blessings through you, then God will get the blessings to you!"

At first, it was difficult to see what she saw from the top of the peak. The truth of the matter was that many of us had been dealt a very ugly deck of cards, often the same cards were passed down to our parents and their parents before them. You'll hear people say things, like "These are the cards I was dealt with," which could very well be the truth. But do yourself a favor and stop repeatedly speaking condescending, self-defeating thoughts out loud. Being dealt with unsatisfactory cards doesn't mean you have to play those cards or the same tired ol' petty games for the rest of your life. You have been blessed with the amazing power to change the deck. In fact, you can change your deck of cards right now! It's a choice, and you have the power to do so. You can choose to see and speak from an eagle's view, and not of a mouse.

There's a big difference between speaking from a winning mindset and one from failure. The same thing goes with being a victim of a crime. We legally become victims when someone violates our life or property. The good news is that you don't have to wear the pain like a badge. At some point, you have to shake that negative energy off of your wings. The next time you find yourself in a depressed state of mind, shake it off with these steps. Imagine that the recent bad news you received was actually the good news you wished for. Think about how happy you would've been and what it would've looked, smelled, and felt like, using as many of your senses as possible. Practice this every time you feel hurt by what has happened. This won't change the reality of the situation; however, it will prevent you from soaking in misery. And more importantly, this practice will prepare you for the comeback.

Your wings have places to go, and new people to see. Look down upon your challenges instead of being looked down on by them. Once you get that dust shaken off, you'll be ready to do what an old-timer once told me many years ago: "It isn't all about what you have but what you do with it." What do you currently have in your hands that you can focus your energy on? Is it an idea for a ground-breaking invention, a new savory recipe, a groundbreaking teaching method, a new global sport franchise, a technology firm manufacturing spaceships, or a futuristic clothing line? You get the point. Whatever it is, remember your journey is a game of chess, not checkers. Plan ahead and be strategic about every move. It's a marathon, not a race. Our past has a lot to do with how we perceive ourselves but not enough to predict our future. You are the master of your fate. The future is created by what we do in the now. When it comes to the past, do your best to only focus on old victories and memories, such as the good times, the smiles, graduations, marriages, and birthdays.

Your current time, space, and actions all are key codes to a cosmic combination that unlocks your destiny. Every good and bad experience and the words you speak, play an essential role in either stopping or pushing you forward to your destiny. When the moment of opportunity presents itself, you must be ready. After all, that is what success is about, right? When preparation meets opportunity, great things happen! Have your business cards, proposal, and flyers ready for that business owner that is around the corner. Get your nonprofit organization documents in order so that when a large donor calls you for a meeting you aren't scrambling. Master your craft in whatever you do best. While most of the world's ideas and products are average, yours will be excelsior. Rise to the occasion, knowing that you deserve better, and go after the victory with the confidence that you've already won. Don't be in such a rush to the top that you miss out on the defining moments that make life worthwhile.

During my teen years in the 90s, it was imperative to have a swagger in our steps. My shirts and pants fit me, my chin was always up, and my back was straight when I sat down. I also showed off a smile that was as bright as the sun. Nowadays, I see many grown men, and even women, walking around lost with their pants halfway past their rear end or with their crotch showing. The correlation between young babies with diapers and these adult-aged people walking with their pants sagging are eerily similar, a product of the agony they were forced to bear, perhaps. A lot of it has to do with a lack of confidence, honor, history of their ancestors, self-respect, and a life filled with often losing. My job is to show you how to mentally turn that lack into abundance. Success isn't hard to come by, if you do your best to obtain it. Get your tickets to ride that train while you still can. ALL ABOARD!

2nd Half

POSITIVE IN, POSITIVE OUT!

The main component of computer science is programming. Computer science isn't my cup of tea. However, as an internet marketing director and search engine optimization (SEO) specialist for twelve years, I've worked with all sorts of digital devices, such as video drones, cameras, computers, and tablets. The information you type into the computer is what the computer spits out to you on the screen. Garbage in, garbage out. Positivity in, positivity out. When we input positive information, we get positive outcomes as a result.

As mentioned earlier, the human brain is a *supercomputer* with nearly one hundred to two hundred billion brain cells. These brain cells, known as neurons, can record, memorize, and create the world around you. The great news here is that you have sovereign power and absolute authority on whether it's going to be a positive or negative atmosphere. This is why it is vitally crucial to input (download) the right types of information into your supercomputer. In a sense, you are either conditioning your mind with positivity or defaulting to negativity until a virus completely wipes out your whole system—losing your mind and dreams in the process. Many of us are on the fence on which type of conditioning we want, but at the end of the day, one side will completely take over. It's all a matter of which part you are feeding the most with your daily actions and words. What type of thoughts do you dwell on most often, positive or negative? Both take the same amount of energy to express, but the latter is taxing on our minds, hearts, and friendships. What type of emotions consumes your day? Joy or Anger? Love or Fear? You can't live by both, eventually one will have to go. This principle also applies to fear and faith. I'd advise you to choose faith. So, how do you go about feeding your faith? Be mindful of how you speak to and about yourself and others during times of despair.

"If it wasn't for bad luck, I wouldn't have any luck at all." "I'll never get that job!" "It can't get any worse than this." That last one is probably the worst thing you can say when you're caught up in an ugly situation. You may be in a bad spot at this very moment; if so, it was a smart decision to read this book. Your troubles will not last forever, and the sun will shine every morning. With every sunrise, there's a new beginning. Regardless of what you're going through, it hasn't failed to rise yet. When you're in an ugly situation, speak as if it has already come to pass, knowing that things will get better. What do you have to lose? Try it! Give your faith in action a chance to turn things around! If it looks like you're losing, why not speak as if you're winning. As the old saying goes, "It ain't over til' it's over!"

Truth be told, most of us don't acknowledge the God in us or even know how to. In our hearts, we pray to a God that is somewhere up in the sky and over the rainbow. <u>There is no God in the sky if there is no God inside.</u> And on top of that, while our heads are down, we're conditioned add to our prayer, "I am not worthy. I don't deserve your goodness." Why even say those things? What power does those words possess? By speaking those types of words, you're already setting yourself up for failure instead of victory. It's understandable that preachers teach us these praying rituals to humble ourselves before the Creator, however, it's my belief that those incantations have a crumbling effect on most of our psyche. The velleity of your prayers and wishes shows that you're not serious enough to take action. I say this because you are putting yourself down by mumbling self-defeating phrases in front of your Creator who has called you to rise up!

God is the ultimate spiritual force and power in the universe so it's alright to be a little beamish while praying, actually, you should be. But instead of kneeling and looking down, stand up and speak up by including encouraging words to your devotions. Start claiming, "I AM more than a conqueror! "I AM worthy. I deserve all of your goodness." I AM the child of the Most High God, the creator of all things! Thank you. I AM going to make you proud for creating me!" You don't have to give grandiloquent devotions every time, but at least make sure that you believe in them yourself. Praying should usually be a joyful experience and never one of doom and gloom.

There are tons of people, rich and poor, that don't believe in God, praying, or that there's a higher power. That doesn't mean that they're bad people, it's just not their cup of tea. Praying is a mind-changing process, you can go from doubt to faith, from hate to love, from fearing to believing, and from losing to winning in a matter of seconds. I'm not talking about one of those quick ten seconds microwave prayers that we do before we eat; deep prayers may take twenty minutes or a couple of hours depending on what level of spiritual connection you're reaching for. It is a positive mental transaction between you and The Creator. Praying is the act of attempting to communicate and connecting with the divinity, the power, the consciousness, and the presence of The Creator and the Inner-G within you. Many of our prayers aren't answered for various reasons; it's my belief that some of the causes are due to the fact that we don't believe in what we're praying for, they're unrealistic, faithless, or have ill intentions. Deep prayers and meditations are both ancient rituals dating back thousands of years; these rituals are so powerful that they both can give you access to another dimension of consciousness and, therefore, create a vortex to a whole new world into your life.

A PRESENT HISTORY

For generations, people of African descent have been taught they're inferior, lazy, and illiterate. There are systems in place to ensure we never stand up or become self-sufficient and self-motivating. We have been sold on the idea of being inherently born criminals and less than our fellow man to the point that we embraced the self-failure image. This has been going on since the slave ships left the African shores with human cargo to stock the plantations with free labor. To add insult to injury, the inhumane institution was upheld within constitutional laws and classrooms across the nation. Overtime, this lead many of us back to the prison plantations, which is modern-day slavery; this proves that just because an act is legal doesn't mean it's right. Time and time again, our ancestors proved that those inferior ideologies were completely wrong despite the enormous opposition. The only reason this tactic seemed to work was due to the fact that fear was inculcated into our mind, physically beaten or burnt unto our bodies with burning hot cow branding irons, and therefore trapped us in the excruciating pain of living a generational nightmare that wouldn't go away.

Ultimately, those events hindered most of our spirits from elevating and advancing—only God knows how the likes of Marry Ellen Pleasant, who started the civil rights movement, and Jean Baptiste Point du Sable, who discovered Chicago, were able to rise up to become extremely wealthy during the madness. Key information, such as our cultural history was withheld, and our names were switched (reprogramming). All of this was done to erase our identity, but you can never eradicate one's DNA of greatness.

Our ancestors lived through countless demeaning and traumatic experiences of every kind imaginable. Distinguished people, like Phyllis Wheatley, Booker T. Washington, Nat Turner, Fredrick Douglass, Annie Malone and her protégé Madame C.J. Walker, and The Honorable Marcus Mosiah Garvey, Jr., to name a few, would go on to make history by defying the odds stacked against them and rising to the top of the world. How was this possible? Simple. They remained positive and refused to give up. Their stories are almost unbelievable but obviously possible to reach a level of success despite their time's insurmountable pressures and challenges.

We have no excuse to give up since they didn't. They had real pressure and problems from stinking thinking from people with guns. As we all know, there was an immense amount of racism during the post-Civil

War era of 1865 leading to the Voting Rights Act of 1965. There was a constant threat of death around every corner. It was nothing short of a miracle that many of them became extremely wealthy and powerful in their own right, not just among the black communities but also in the white communities. This is especially true for General Francois-Dominique Toussaint L'Ouverture, who was possibly the first multimillionaire of African descent in the Western hemisphere owning multiple pieces of property and a plethora of horses. Booker T. Washington rose to prominence and was invited to the White House in 1901 to sit with former President Theodore Roosevelt and the first lady.[22] It's a very high honor to be invited to the White House and even more so during the height of deadly racial injustices and prejudices in the United States. The Negro Spirituals that were sung on the slave plantations all across the blazing hot cotton, sugar cane, and tobacco fields that kept the God in them alive. I'm convinced that those soulful songs helped them maintain their hope, culture, and sanity in their living nightmare.

General Toussaint L'Ouverture, an African-Haitian leader in the Haitian Revolutionary War against the French and British from 1791 to 1803. He was an exemplary soldier, entrepreneur, and skilled statesman. He was able to remind the world that African people were highly intelligent and despised being enslaved. The current school system programmed our minds to label our African ancestors as slaves. They shouldn't be called that because we were so much more. From the 16th to 19th century much as 100 million people were kidnapped and terrorized from Africa, during the Atlantic Slave Trade's Middle Passage, to work against their will in different parts of the world depending on the colonizer's country.[23] 80 million of them, or so, didn't survive the initial stages of the horrific Middle Passage's 5,000 mile chained voyage,

[22] Eliot Brown, "Guest of Honor: : Booker T. Washington, Theodore Roosevelt, and the White House Dinner That Shocked a Nation" by Deborah Davis," *Today I Found Out*, July 17, 2012, https://www.washingtonpost.com/guestofhonor
[23] Dr. Huggins, Nathan Irvin. "Black Odyssey: The Afro-American Ordeal in Slavery" First Edition 1977. NY: Pantheon Books, 1977.

which is now officially known as the African Holocaust. These people were human beings who were taken and sold as human cargo.[24] A few of them were even royalty yet stripped of their titles and dignity. The fact that General Toussaint defeated the mighty French, Spaniards, Americans, and British armies makes him a real-life superhero. Many believe he had super powers, especially when fighting fiercely on his horse during a battle. By playing these powerful countries against each other was sheer brilliance, further evidence that he rejected the programming and indoctrination of inferiority. He always found a way to win.

General Toussaint's success goals did not only manifest, but they embarrassed the top nations of the eighteenth and nineteenth centuries. He defeated the odds, along with some African-Haitian soldiers, and won one of the biggest wars in history. This one victory placed European countries and the United States on notice that evils of chattel slavery were coming to an end. It wasn't a matter of if it would cease, but when. The global propaganda that people of African descent were inferior, lazy, and illiterate was finally proven to be false. Haiti was the first and only country established after a successful revolt of enslaved people.

This one act of courage by brave Africans would change the course of history worldwide forever; this event changed the consciousness of those who were in shackles to demand their freedom, as well. Nat Turner, the charismatic preacher, is a perfect example. Once he read an article about the Haitian Revolution, along with a solar eclipse, he was motivated to do the same. He led the most memorable rebellion for freedom by enslaved Africans on American soil on August 21, 1831, in Southampton, Virginia. They wrote themselves into the history books. This dark part of history saddens most people; however, I find their perseverance motivating. It's the mindfulness of knowing

---

[24] Clarke, John Henrik. Christopher Columbus and the Afrikan Holocaust: Slavery and the Rise of European Capitalism. Eworld. New York. 1992

what your ancestors stood up for that gives you power. I'm inspired to work diligently and in excellence towards what I want out of life. Did you know that on most plantations that people were whipped to work twenty-three-hour shifts, and that pregnant women worked on the fields until it was time to deliver their child? This is the sole reason why I never complain when I find myself working twelve hard hours for my own company.

Ask yourself: What am I going to stand up against and stand up for?

Knowing there is a god in you is one thing but speaking and invoking that power is a whole different ballgame since you're giving yourself a natural advantage. Embracing your Inner-G is equivalent to turning your grandma's station wagon into a Transformer. Acknowledging that you can speak of a good life of wholeness, healing, excellent health, loving relationships, and financial prosperity makes you incredibly wealthy in spirit and truth. Being taught for generations that money is evil and sinful has placed many of us in a regressive state of mind, turning us into poverty thinking beings.

Over time, we've developed a Rejection Complex, which makes us consciously deny and reject that anything good can or will come our way. We've convinced ourselves that we don't deserve to be happy, wealthy, or have favor in our lives. Many of us have been down and out for so long, we've convinced ourselves that being the underdog and scratching our heads on the first of every month is the only life we'll have. That's a sad sack of potatoes. Growing up we were taught that power was of the devil. What they didn't tell us is that the lack of power places us in the devil's den where all types of ill thoughts and demonic spirits resides. Well...power is a part of life and everything around us is based on it. You can't move forward or live without power, just like a battery without power is useless, since a car can't move forward without it. For a person without money or power is stepped on, and looked down upon. Good health, peace of mind, high self-worth, and happiness are among the things that make us truly rich. Get more power! Or you'll get ran over by those with power that wish you ill will.

Caged Eagles Can't Fly

In China, there's a zoo with a bald eagle named Baeksul that couldn't fly to save his life. He doesn't even attempt to flap its wings and walks everywhere he goes. Yes, he looks like an eagle, smells like an eagle, yet acts and walks like a penguin.[25] Baeksul even runs away from giant worms that he's being fed, and is petrified of snakes, which is normally a juicy snack for his species. Eagles mainly eat larger prey such as squirrels, rabbits, fish, and mice in the wild. The zookeepers unknowingly crippled the eagle's future by hand-feeding it its entire life instead of allowing him to exercise his brainpower to hunt and figure things out on his own. This happens to people when governments spoon-feed an impoverished population instead of showing them how to be self-sufficient with the proper education so they can fish for themselves, the handout regresses self-willingness, and is disempowering. The brains of both humans and wild animals have mental muscles that need regular exercise, or our thinking, acting, and overall living conditions will suffer.

In Baeksul's mind, he doesn't even know he's an eagle. He doesn't know who he is or the fact that he's the king of the skies. It will be nearly impossible for him to mate since the queen eagles are choosy lovers. The female eagle selects her king after he passes a series of flight and strength tests. Baeksul can't fly

[25] SBS TV. 2019, July 13. "Bald Eagle Doesn't Want To Fly, Just Walk Like A Dog LOL." https://www.youtube.com/watch?v=QqDHGnBEdMc. YouTube.

and is limited to walking on the ground, therefore, eliminating himself from the race of love. Eagles, such as the African fish eagle or the golden eagle, are extremely competitive from birth. They're motivated by seeing their peers soar to higher heights. Even though they don't fly in flocks, they watch each other with the ability to see eight miles in every direction.

Eventually, the zookeepers decided to bring in a few eagles to motivate and train Beaksul, but he wasn't moved at all. It was too late. The damage to his psyche and physical body was already done.

People suffer from all types of illnesses and traumas that can destroy them mentally and physically unless something is consciously done. We've all lost a job before, and it sucks to be unemployed for long periods of time. There's no reason why our faith should be unemployed. Give your faith a job! What do you have to lose? Faith is no good until you have faith in yourself. The essential thing in this life is to believe in you. Believe in the presence and power of God, the Infinite Divine Energy within yourself. Your entire experience is based on it. Once you believe in your goals, it's much easier to invest in yourself. Invest in your education to push you further along your upcoming illustrious career. Invest in a life coach to help improve your self-worth and self-esteem if you have to. Invest in a psychologist that can help you in the healing process, if necessary. Invest in books that can guide you towards making a substantial financial increase, or in whatever area you lack wisdom in. This is how the smart stays smart.

As part of your Mental Makeover, when you're sick or injured, you must stop cursing the injury. "My bad shoulder", "my bad leg", or "I have a messed-up life". The same goes for speaking to people. "Those bad kids" or "my deadbeat dad". These condescending words and thoughts aren't going to activate the desired outcomes or even give miracles a chance to manifest.

Speak this into the atmosphere instead:

"I have great health and happiness; therefore, I AM rich. I AM beautiful. I AM loved. I AM greater than the challenges before me. I AM. I AM. I AM!"

"God is in the miracle-working business" was one of Reverend Ike's (Frederick J. Eikerenkoetter II) most popular sayings. He once shared a story of a woman, let's call her Sherry, that was on welfare for twenty-four years while raising six children. She sacrificed to make it to one of the reverend's conferences in Los Angeles. Sherry had a hard time receiving the knowledge that there was a God or even a higher power within her. She eventually took action on Reverend Ike's teachings and prayed to God boldly, "Please show me my gifts. Show me my talents!" Eventually, she felt the voice of The Creator tell her, "Well, you raised six children. That is your gift and talent. You are a professional childcare specialist!"

From that day forth, she told her friends and neighbors that were on welfare that she was a childcare specialist. She began claiming her new title, and just as important, she began to walk in her purpose by putting her faith in action. She was eager to not only share her success but help the single mothers in her community by motivating them to get off the Welfare Plantation. She was able to help them get better jobs by babysitting their children for free, but only if they were going to job interviews. Her popularity grew so much from her success in getting mothers off welfare that the city certified her as a childcare specialist. Monetary donations came pouring in from sponsorships from multiple companies and from people she never met. A university even gave her an honorary doctorate in childcare specialization. All of this happened because she acknowledged her Inner-G, self-worth, and walked in her purpose in serving others. We all have gifts and talents, regardless of our socio-economic situation. Allow me to let you in on a secret—your finances don't determine who you are, or how great you'll become. To find out how great you can be, seriously ask yourself.

"God in me, show me how to use my talents now.
Show me what to do with what gifts you've given me?
How can I be a blessing to my family and community?
Show me how to prosper!"

There is something great you can do that no one else can do like you. A brain may be a terrible thing to squander, but skipping out on your talent, whether it's producing movies, hosting a talk show, writing books, or teaching, is a travesty. The opportunities to pursue your passions will fade away if you don't act on your dreams. Your goals will remain notional ideas unless you willfully pursue them into existence. No one wants to be that person kicking rocks down the road, sounding like a broken record. It's bad energy to constantly speak about all of the dreams and ideas that you failed to go after. Tomorrow isn't guaranteed to anyone. You either use it or lose it. Many of us give up without even giving ourselves a shot at presenting our gifts to the world, especially if we're struggling financially. There is always a way if there is a will in you to find it.

In addition, John Mosley, husband, father, and the celebrity basketball coach at East Los Angeles College, said it best, "Excuses are tools the incompetent use to build monuments of nothing!" People that use them freely rarely amount to anything but a lifetime of sorrow. The poor, lazy, and evil will always be amongst us, but that doesn't mean you have to be one of them. Your gift could be what allows your family to have the financial breakthrough that all of you have been waiting for. You can depend on hitting the winning numbers in your state's lottery if you'd like, or you can have the odds on your side for a change. How? By speaking up and putting your Inner-G to work while burning the midnight oil.

What's a common way to wake up someone that's sleeping? You call them, right? Well then, call up your greatness by encouraging yourself. CLAP YOURSELF HAPPY! Keep clapping until you feel your mood has improved. It doesn't have to be a loud and obnoxious clap but hard enough that you can feel the energy in your hands saturate the atmosphere. Your happiness is an invaluable component to your quality of life. Heaven isn't up in the clouds somewhere. Heaven is right here, right now. You have the choice of deciding whether you want to live in Hell on Earth or Heaven today! On April 15, 2011, I started a journal entitled *King Kevin's Dreams*. Within it are seventy-one of my written dreams and goals. Years ago, I started with twenty goals after I had the pleasure of listening to Terri Foy, an inspirational speaker and author from Texas. During a leadership conference, Mrs. Foy came to my church to encourage us to visualize our goals and believe in our dreams. This stunning, small-framed, squeaky-voiced woman blessed us with powerful instructions that left a positive impact on our lives, even to this day.

"See with the eyes of faith. Speak what you see in the spiritual realm until you see it in the natural," she told the audience. "The ideas come first, and the visions come second!"

Pulling our ideas into the physical realm is extremely powerful, and it's a lesson I shall never forget. Every creative idea that has manifested was a thought before it became a reality. I am excited to teach you how to pull those ideas into reality into the physical realm during the upcoming chapters. The art of visualization and seeing the world with your third eye, "spiritual eyes" or "eyes of faith" will give you access to a whole new world, which leads to a new and improved version of you. I've been using the power of my spiritual eyes ever since I first learned about it. The list expanded to seventy-one goals, in which fifteen of my dreams have been accomplished; I cross them out just enough so that I can still see and read them out loud with the rest of the goals to remind me to continue being ambitious; this keeps me mentally hungry, and not complacent with a handful of victories. Reprogramming your mind out of the plantation ideology isn't an option, it's a must if you're going to spread your eagle wings!

Nothing is impossible to a mind organized in positive belief. It's imperative to get your mind right. Once you do that, you can work toward getting your heart in order, for it is written, "Keep your heart with all diligence, for out of it are the issues of life." When the heart, mind, and gut are in one accord, you will access the keys that unlocks the secret powers of visualization, opening the portal to manifestation. For many years, you've been trying your best to accomplish certain goals, but you're missing the key ingredient of visualization. It could've been that your heart wasn't into what your mind was thinking, while your gut wasn't in agreement.

Do what Floyd 'Money' Mayweather, Jr. does—he over trains for most of his fights. He keeps practicing his boxing skills until his entire being is in agreement. Money Mayweather was also known to leave night clubs jogging home instead of driving one of his superfluity of foreign cars (owning over 100 vehicles), thanks to his flawless boxing record his career earnings are over $1 billion dollars and counting. What does he know about winning? The undefeated billion-dollar boxer only thrashed sixteen world champions in sixteen consecutive fights. The cherry on top, he's now a 'retired' boxer that never really quit fighting and is the CEO of his own boxing promotion company; he'll set up a fight for hundreds of millions of dollars, promote it through his company, win the fight, and then cash in on both sides of the table. He bought his self out of a contract for $750,000 to buy his self out of boxing promoting contract from Top Ranks. This enabled him to not have to wait or depend on how much they wanted to pay him. That small $750,000 investment was a self-promotional chess move that allowed him to make $750,000,000 in just three block buster fights. Now that's what I call a "green print" that is worth following! He knew that he was the best even though major television network producers believed that he had an inflated self-evaluation of his worth. Now, Mr. Mayweather, with his 50-0 perfect record, literally writes his own checks. If you think like a rodent, you'll easily eat crumbs all day, but when you think like a lion, you'll end up with the lion's share.

For reemphasis purposes, in order to become a successful imagineer, you have to actively utilize the power of visualization. Use your dream home as an example. Picture living in a beautiful three-level home with eight bedrooms and five bathrooms with a jacuzzi bathtub in each, a double walk-in closet with an island in the middle with mirrors in every corner, an air-conditioned four-car garage, and a large yard on all sides with plenty of space for different styles of patio furniture to sit on and enjoy based on the sun's position. Breathe deep and smell the fragrance of a South Beach five-star hotel, feel the marble counter tops in the kitchen, and imagine your tired muscles loosening in a custom made jacuzzi pool to relax in. Visualize walking into your dream home daily, and the rest shall follow. If you can visualize it, you can achieve it so GO GET IT!

VISUALIZATION EXERCISE

1. Write down your top ten most desirable dreams/goals.
2. Choose one of your dreams and visualize it by using your five gates (sight, touch, smell, hearing, and taste) with as much depth as possible.
3. Breathe deeply and slowly for 5-10 minutes (when possible), especially during Step #2.
4. Repeat these steps two to three times a day—every day. Please, don't rush any of these steps because your body needs time to absorb the effects of each one.

Now, practice your new mental exercise with your brand spanking new dream car. Start and rev the engine of your new car in your mind. Change the car's color several times from red to green, then black to pink to yellow. While you're at it, try camouflaging it. Flip the interior too. Add stripes to it, rims as big and shiny as you want them, a drop-top, or even a hardtop. How does the leather seats smell? Does it have the new car smell or can you smell your favorite air freshener? Don't forget to add lotion on the tires. Changing the features in your mind is good visualization practice for more meaningful things and can be lots of fun in other meaningful ways. This is true power.

Don't stop there! Let us do the same with your financial security. No money, no honey! We all feel better when our money is right. In your mind, sign the contract for your new six-figure salary. How are you dressed for your first day at work? How does your new office look? Feel the sensation of the fancy chair at your oakwood desk as you imagine sitting in it for the first time.

If you want to open a business let's imagine that you're opening a restaurant. How are you dressed for the opening day? How are you greeting your chefs or your customers? Visualize the design of the menu or how the fragrance of the food smells. Is it spicy, baked, or fried? Make it what you want because people who are passionate about what they are doing bring about greater success for themselves, since the sky is the limit. Nobody knows how far you can go. Those that are stuck to the employment standards of a 9 to 5 can only hope for limited success.

This visualization practice can work wonders for other dreams and goals as well. If you wish to play on a sports team, even professionally, take time to see yourself being offered the position you want for the sports team you've been training so hard for. If you enjoy music, create your own world-famous orchestra with you as the world-renowned composer. Can you see and feel the elegant suit or dress you would wear as you bow in front of the audience? Can you now see what I see?

Visualization is limitless and it helps to transport our dreams from the spiritual realm into the present so we can make them our reality!

Organize your thoughts and aim towards the direction that you want your life to go in. Know that the blessings you need come from believing and knowing what belongs to you by working smart for it. There are no free rides, and there's a slim chance that someone is just going to give it to you.

Final Thoughts

It's a constant battle to remain positive, yet it's achievable, on the condition that you truly believe deep down inside that you will win. A winning mindset does not give up on hope. Put in the "burning the midnight oil" type of effort to see your victory to the end. Tough times will come and that's when you'll discover things about yourself that you never really knew were possible. Remember to direct your billions of brain cells toward your dreams and passions daily, and you'll reach the success you envisioned. It's only a matter of time, providing that, you've put in the necessary work to manifest your desired reality. All of which is made possible because you've made it your business to get your ducks in a row.

5 STEPS TO START YOUR MENTAL MAKEOVER

Step One: Practice the following with your thoughts: Positive in, positive out.

Step Two: Believe in yourself (even if you really don't).

Step Three: Dump your negative attitude in order to reach a higher altitude.

- Say something nice when you find yourself complaining or feeling like being mean to someone.

Step Four: Walk out your ideas in your mind first before writing your plan. Also, include your after the victory plan. Every detail counts.

Step Five: See your victory. Taste your victory. Go get your victory!

Special Note:

In regard to procrastination, the imaginary feelings of success that you're able to conjure up will motivate you to push through and overcome your real-life resistance to accomplish what needs to be done. Your feelings are real, and you should use them as jet fuel to reach your destination.

DIVINE ENERGY AND INTELLIGENCE

TO DREAM OR
NOT TO DREAM

HERE ARE FOUR TRAGEDIES IN LIFE. THE FIRST IS not to reach your heart's desire. The second is finding success without a plan and losing it. The third is not knowing who you are, and the fourth is not dreaming at all. The first step in avoiding the initial tragedy is by understanding who you are is based on acknowledging that your mind is your most valuable asset. By now, you know your brain is a supercomputer with billions of brain cells that must be programmed for a specific purpose. Our dreams can supply us with that purpose in the means of signs and symbols if we know how to interpret them after we've awakened from our deep state of sleep. This can be accomplished by documenting and studying your dreams.

With that being said, the first computer on Earth was the brain's subconscious mind. Your mind must be activated to organize itself and perform a specific function based on your level of intelligence, comprehension, consciousness, and direction. Our African ancestors of Kemet understood the science of brain data better than any civilization of the past ever did, perhaps even with today's technology.

Perhaps this knowledge resulted from thousands of years of research, building, trial and error, dreams, prayers, and the secret powers of meditation. With the consciousness of divine minds working together and the collective power of unity in their communities, our ancestors possessed an incredible amount of spiritual and organizational skills that made them extremely powerful and wealthy in their own right. It's also noteworthy that the mental strength of the ancients gave them the fortitude to build over four hundred pyramids throughout the regions of Kush (Ancient Ethiopia) and Kemet (Ancient Egypt). For centuries, the Great Pyramid of Giza has boggled the minds of scholars, professors, and scientists, so much so that the powers that be created a study around the African culture called Egyptology.[26]

How in the heavens did this ancient civilization know how to create such magnificent structures with laser cutting precision and technology that can't be duplicated in the 21st century? One thing is for sure: it started in their spirit. Thanks to trailblazing scholars, such as, Imhotep, the world's first multi-genius and surgeon, and possibly the greatest intellect to ever walk the planet, was able to utilize the power of his mind and metric rulers. To his credit, most history scholars and Egyptologists believe Imhotep spearheaded the planning and execution of the Pyramids of Giza, named after three Kings: Khufu, Khafre, and Menkaure — to correspond with the powerful leaders for whom they were constructed. The second and largest of the trio is entitled the Great Pyramid, and was built during the 4th dynasty (2580-2560 BCE).[27] It somehow is still standing today, thousands of years later. Each side measures 755.752ft and it stands at 4814ft. In fact, it's the only edifice out of the Seven Wonders of the Ancient World that still exists.

[26] Joshua, J. Mark. Great Pyramid Of Giza. Published On December 19, 2016. Ancient History Encyclopedia. https://www.ancient.eu/great_pyramid_of_giza/
[27] Dr. Diop, Cheikh Anta, Cook, Mercer. "The African Origin of Civilization Myth or Realty." (1974 - Lawrence Hill Books.), 86

Wouldn't it be excellent to be able to tap into your mind's superpowers and build upon your ancestor's legacy with something that will last for generations? Wouldn't you be better off using your mindpower for more useful purposes than punching the time clock at a job you resent every day? Your answer should be a resounding YES! Make your life count.

"In Your Dreams"

Are you having dreams of soaring through the air? Surrounded by water? According to dream therapists, flying dreams, mean that you'll have an opportunity to rise above a situation for a much-needed new perspective. They can also mean the dreamer wants to escape or avoid dealing with something difficult in their life. Speaking of difficulties, a drastic change in your life can be depicted in your dream or nightmare because of the dramatic way your life has been impacted. The good news is that the bad dreams aren't necessarily precognitive of what's to come; instead, they're a reaction to what has occurred or currently happening in your life. As a result, for many of us, it causes us to wake up on the wrong side of the bed. You can do something about it or continue sleeping on it. No pun intended.

Furthermore, there are cultures of the past and present that partake in interesting rituals in a search for a sign to make major decisions. For example, shaking animal bones on the ground, bird signs (formations), the shape of the moon, or the weather to determine what will be their next move. Whether it be to go to war or seek peace, sell their land, or to go hunting, they know it could very well be their last adventure. So, if you think that using your dreams to help with your decision-making is farfetched, think again.

Dreams are seeds of things to come. The innerstanding of your visions could be the vehicle to physically connect you to your future. [The present creates the future against the echoes of the past.] Love yourself enough to continue to dream. They hold the keys to the combination safe that's holding the multimillion-dollar ideas you have stored away deep within your subconscious. Dreams create desires, which leads to expectations and opens the gateway to the one thing that will wake up the sleeping giant inside us: our imagination. Dreams are also a way of gaining the self-awareness and energy we need to prosper. 33% to 35% of our dreams are possible because they come true if you understand what they mean; dreams allow us to focus energy in a specific direction instead of all over the place. 12% to 15% of our dreams may even predict the future.[28] It makes perfect sense that both the conscious and subconscious mind working together can bring our dreams to fruition, as long as we're willing to put in the elbow grease. Although scientists have not validated that dreams come true, however, they use terms like precognitive dreams or premonitions.[29]

"Imagination is more important than knowledge. Logic will get you from point A to point B; imagination will get you everywhere!"

ALBERT EINSTEIN

The imagination is the most marvelous powerful force we all have. Daydreaming expresses the degree of imagination that we possess as individuals; since it's also a phenomenal mental faculty that is often connected with anticipating the future, we usually think of it in a fantasy context. We are in a physical world using our faculties to get what we need and want; it's a matter of wanting beyond life's basic necessities. On the positive side, we're all equipped with perception,

---

[28] Richmond, Cynthia, "Dream Power," 30. Simon & Schuster, New York, NY.
[29] Ibid., 22.

will, memory, intuition, and imagination. All of this is good stuff. It's more than good—it's great! On the negative side, we're not taught how to utilize these natural gifts. Consequently, the average person tiptoes through life, hoping to peacefully find their grave without ever reaching their fullest potential or seeing their dreams manifest. It's safe to say that we all want to be more than average and beyond common. Everyone has an imagination, yet some are larger than others. Fortunately, there are those that have mastered the power of imagination to a higher degree, thus making them filthy rich by using their energy purposely towards reaching their mark, thus creating a god-like aura.

This power can be seen leaving your body with Kirlian photography (invented in 1939 by Semyon Davidovich Kirlian), which is a photography process that reveals visible "auras" around the objects, animals, and you guessed it—people.[30] This same powerful energy flows to and from our minds and heart. At this point, we can consciously control the vibration, or bioenergy, of the human body which emits low-level light, heat, and acoustical energy. These are electrical and magnetic properties working together to create your personal biofield.[31] Consider your body as its own personal ecosystem—you can either pollute it with toxic energy and wasteful thoughts, or keep it clean with good energy and positive actions. The more positivity you create from your imagination the stronger your god-like aura becomes as you reach new levels of success, power, and kindness. People tend to flock towards those that exhibit special knowledge and/or wealth with a proven track record. This is why experts within a certain field publish books, and with efficient marketing, become bestsellers. Their book tours, LIVE videos, and lectures are always packed due to the fact that their supporters want to

---

[30] Towne, Rachael. "What is Kirlian Photography? Aura Photography Revealed." Updated, January 22, 2020. https://www.lightstalking.com/what-is-kirlian-photography-the-science-and-the-myth-revealed/

[31] Dr. Rubik, Beverly, "Measurements of the Human Biofield and Other Energic Instruments." https://www.faim.org/measurement-of-the-human-biofield-and-other-energetic-instruments

THE WINNER IN THE MIRROR

be as close as possible to their aura. Since the beginning of time, there has always been a market for those thirsty for knowledge. As companies improve the creative ways that the world consumes knowledge, technology continues to advance over time, however, the fact remains the same—knowledge is power.

There are two threats to our success, imagination, happiness, and prosperity. The primary and most common is fear, which carries a level of direful energy that no one wants to be around; the exact opposite of those that possess the benevolent power of the god-like aura. As humans, we are creatures of routines, and as we get older, it becomes harder to break out of old habits. A change of environment can cause fear in some and a sense of joy and peace of mind in others. Case in point, the mountain of relief you get when you're able to escape an abusive or dreadful relationship. We all can recall the jubilant sensation after passing a final exam. Believe it or not, some people fear success or even becoming wealthy. Have you ever seen *Brewster's Millions*, the 1985 comedy film starring Richard Pryor and John Candy? In the film, Richard went stir-crazy when he went from barely making ends meet to catching a break of a lifetime with an unexpected $300 million inheritance. But the catch was that he had to spend exactly $30 million in thirty days with no possessions or interest from the investments to his name at the end of the month in order to inherit the whole shebang! Spending a million bucks a day sounds easy, right? It's nearly impossible not to gain any interest in your investments with that level of capital. Ladies & gentlemen, that's how the rich stay rich!

Richard didn't know what to do with himself, and he couldn't spend the money fast enough. Throughout the movie, he feared he would lose his friends, the inheritance, and his mind until he came back to his senses that it was just money. It was at that point that he realized what was really important, which was his peace of mind and the genuine love his friends had for each other. Once again, love saved the day. Not the piles of cash, cars, or clothes. After that, the paranoia of being wealthy and lonely went away.

The Magic behind Visualization

Visualization practices allow you to clarify the good you desire and deserve. Whatever idea you make clear in your mind and take the <u>proper actions</u> towards must happen. Visualization gives your mind's eye work to do by pressing your thoughts upon the subconscious mind. The subconscious mind takes whatever idea is impressed upon it and materializes it so you can clearly see it. To make it big in this life, you need out-of-the-box, constructive, productive, creative, and positive ideas. Dreams and daydreams allow you to unlock the mysteries of the mind by tapping into your limitless subconscious mind.

The images we build in our minds dictate the vibrations our temple operates in. Conscious-level vibrations are our feelings. It's important to <u>hold onto positive images of how you want to live in your mind with your deepest feelings and all of your might</u>—it's your feelings attached to the vision that truly gets you the blessings. Make the choice to live, walk, and talk towards the direction you're hoping for until it manifests!

Fear has a death gripping effect on peoples' creativity, dreams, and will cause us to not even try, let alone take one confident step toward our purpose. This is why fear is Public Enemy #1. If you can take one step then you can take two steps towards accomplishing your dreams. Then three steps, then four steps, so on, and so forth. Once you get your ducks in a row and get the ball rolling in a positive direction it will be hard to stop your progress. Afterall, success is an accumulation of small, positive actions, done repeatedly.

As an illustration, being close enough to hear a lion's roar is a great reason to be afraid. Lions have a polarizing effect on people, but the majority of us will never see a lion up close, outside of a zoo, so what are you so afraid of? Consider fear as an illusion, a manifested lie, self-created, and is usually influenced by outside entities. A lion or tiger can roar as loud as 114 decibels and can be heard a distance of five miles away. It is about twenty-five times louder than a gas-powered lawnmower. The loudness of a tiger's roar shakes the body of its prey hard enough to paralyze them. The situations in life that we face are nowhere near as frightening as a tiger or lion, yet we crumble at our bills, evening news, bullies, and sadly, our future. Fear has a paralyzing power that can and will lead you to a poverty-stricken life, mindset, and spirit, but only if you allow it to. This is chiefly why it's utterly important to feed your faith by taking at least one bold step every day possible towards crossing off the tasks listed on your M.A.P. to reach your goals.

While we're on the topic, did you know that there's a name created for every phobia there is? You'd be surprised of the things people are afraid of. Truth be told, I used to suffer from Aporophobia, the fear of becoming poor. After years of consistent hard work and dedication, that thought doesn't even cross my mind. Glossophobia, or speech anxiety, is the fear of public speaking. Arachnophobia or spider phobia refers to the intense fear of spiders. Acrophobia is an excessive fear of heights and manifests as severe anxiety. Believe it or not, there are people that suffer from the fear of becoming wealthy, Plutophobia; the origin of the word comes from Pluto, who was the Roman God of Wealth. Thanks to the COVID-19 quarantine, nearly the entire population of the world has developed germaphobia, which is a pathological fear of contamination and germs. Many times, these fears can overwhelm a person to the point that they can't move; they can be debilitating and interfere with your life.

I've successfully inundated my mind's eye with so much positivity that fear has been washed away from my heart into a bottomless pit. The only thing I fear now is myself when I push beyond my own set of limits to win. How? I was empowered by reading edifying books that I devoted time to study and implement so I could accomplish my worthwhile dreams; both of which dismantled my fears of lack with a two-punch combination—faith and action. Surrounding myself with people who loved me solidified my sunny disposition, and made me want to live my best life even more. We all must strive to live a good life of peace and tranquility, making it easy to share that precious energy with those around us; it's during this time that we discover what we truly love to do. For everything is energy, and energy is everything.

Speaking of which, I realized how much I loved collecting and studying art at museums. Over the years I've visited the top museums in the world, such as the ginormous British Museum in London, Tutankhamun aka King Tut's and the Golden Age of the Pharaohs Exhibit (hosted at the NSU Art Museum Fort Lauderdale), and several mansions that were transformed historic museums throughout the states; rich old people would often give their properties over to the state as a gift to avoid their beloved home from being demolished by wealthy real-estate developers. I got tired of having to go to museums to see paintings, so I hung up paintings with vibrant colors and intriguing details. I also included pictures of those dearest to my heart within my home and office that inspired me. In a sense I turned my living space into a museum.

Ever since I can remember there was a passion in me for reading so eventually, I started to build my own library too. My collection is filled with best-sellers, local authors, and extremely rare old books published as far back as the 1820s. You'll be amazed by how much encouragement you can empower yourself with by simply taking the time to read about the wisdom from trailblazers of the past. Knowledge is definitely power. Thank God for shows like Reading Rainbow that challenged children to read and to utilize their imagination every day. Life would be so boring without ingenuity. Perhaps, you can mirror my steps in using paintings and books to eradicate your fears, and activate your courage.

———

"Knowledge is power. Wisdom is experience."
PASTOR STEPHEN DARBY

———

The second threat to the future you desire is fatigue, better yet, weariness. People get weary all the time. They become tired of dreaming, tired of trying their best and getting the short end of the stick, tired of getting up to only be knocked down again, tired of fighting to keep their lackluster relationship, tired of investors saying no to their business plan, and etc. Life is unpredictable, and can be unfair. There are many variables, such as the economy, employment status, pandemics, government meltdowns, love life, health, and family. With all of its uncertainties, it's almost impossible to stay energized with the constant ups and downs on top of the high and low tidal waves.

Tale of The Double F's

Fear and fatigue are two cousins that feed off each other like hyenas. They need a host to feed on so that they can survive. Eventually, you will make the decision that you have had enough of the Double Fs. You'll also realize they are just two bullies that prey on those they perceive as weak and vulnerable for attack. Fear and fatigue will smell your insecurities, past hurts, and mental weaknesses if they are given time and rent-free space in your brain to develop a negative strength within your character. How? Negativity has a powerful aroma that can become intoxicating. The gloomier your energy, the more you'll begin to smell like a fish that has been out of the water too long and is easy to find.

The Double Fs will jump on every opportunity to attack you like two heat-seeking missiles from a fighter jet. Heat-seeking missiles use infrared light emissions from a target to track and follow targets at a supersonic speed. The US military's AIM 9 Sidewinder fighter aircraft missile, for example, shoots out at 7,500 mph, which is 10 times faster than the speed of sound.[32] Anyone with $603,871 to blow can buy one. I seriously doubt there's a buy-one get-one-free deal though. Targets give off powerful thermal energy, which allows the missile to locate and eliminate it on the ocean, land, or in the sky. As long as you remain negative, fearful, and timid, missiles (dream killers, manipulators, naysayers, haters, or etc.) will continue to track you until you are down and out. The only way to escape them is to not give them a warm target to hit since, in a fearful state, we're vulnerable to be attacked. Timid people are wired to hide, flee, and take flight. Running away from challenges stops here! Be bold. Be courageous. Be hungry.

How does one go from being timid to bold? Good question. First, start by addressing those past hurts by strengthening and fortifying your three brains, particularly your mind and your solar plexus (your gut). See yourself doing things, within reason, you would normally be afraid to do. Your new confidence will leave a sweet-smelling aroma on you that will overpower the stench of fear.

Fear and fatigue roamed the city streets and neighbor-hoods, discouraging and terrifying everyone they came across. They would knock on doors while disguising themselves as salesmen, and when people willingly opened their doors, Fear and Fatigue would knock them to the ground. Once inside,

---

[32] Goldberg, Sam, "Infrared Countermeasures: The Systems That Cool The Threat From Heat-Seeking Missiles," Air & Space Magazine, July 2003. https://www.airspacemag.com/how-things-work/infrared-countermeasures-4739633/

they would pillage the homes, flip the couches, yanking out the dresser and kitchen drawers and emptying their contents on the floor. They would smash all the mirrors and windows, and completely ransack the residences as if they were the FBI searching for drugs and stacks of cash in the walls. They successfully turned these people's lives upside down, snatching their joyful spirits as well. Fear and Fatigue continued doing this for years, and eventually, they grew to a size and confidence no one could stop.

They went from street to street, home to home, church to church, school to school, city to city, state to state, and country to country. There was no end to their pillaging as they stole people's hopes, dreams, and futures, selling them on the black market to the highest bidder. Until one day, they noticed a bright, yellow house on the intersection of Victory Road and More Than a Conqueror Drive radiating with beautiful orchids, sunflowers, and roses, with a yellow brick road leading to their smoked glass double doors. Fear and Fatigue looked at each other and said, "Jackpot, this is the house we've been dreaming about!" They rushed to the estate with lightning speed and banged on the glass doors a few times, but there was no answer. They kept banging and knocking on the door like police detectives for a couple of minutes. Finally, Courage and Faith answered the door after they were done praying. When they opened the door, no one was there. You see, when Faith and Courage show up, Fear and Fatigue disappear.

Nevertheless, it's a constant battle to stay ahead or even afloat, which can leave any of us completely drained of any aspirations to keep moving forward. This sometimes causes people to fall into the quicksand of quitting and thus they drown in doubt, losing the will to even get out of bed in the morning. The biggest battle is the mental fights from within. This is one battle you cannot fail to keep sight of or take lightly. There is an all-out war for the control of your mind from governments, online influencers, and in some cases, even your companion could be trying to manipulate you into making disempowering decisions.

Once you've allowed your mind or spirit to be taken over, all hope is lost; that is why in the very first chapter of this book we discussed how to fortify your mind since it's the foundation on which everything you do and will become is based — and I do mean everything. Your mind is your greatest asset. It must be protected and receive proper daily exercise in order to serve you. The fortification of your mind is tantamount to having your safety deposit boxes secured in a large bank safe; the only way anyone can get in is if you let them in. Allowing someone to bind you mentally and/or spiritually is like a country selling its main water source to a foreign government—it must be avoided by all means! It makes no sense. No one would do such a thing unless they were paid handsomely to sell out their homeland, or lacked the wisdom on what the ramifications would be. Manipulation prevention is a perfect reason why you must replenish your mind, body, and spirit consistently. You'll be able to sniff out the B.S. from the snakes, sharks, and hyenas the moment you sense it, which enables you to act accordingly with the proper chess move. Allowing yourself not to be played.

When you treasure your divinity by acknowledging the divine infinite knowledge and power of your Inner-G, places you a thousand steps ahead of the rest that don't. Depending on the situation, when everything isn't going your way, it's imperative to find the time to be calm, pray, meditate, eat a balanced meal, and strategize — in that order. If you can't find the time, then create it. You were created to create. At times, you may feel as if there is no point and that no one believes in you, but you're wrong! Find someone that believes in you, and their energy, along with their faith, will boost yours. Together, we're going to reverse that stinking thinking. And by the way, I believe in you.

Here are some words of wisdom you can tap into: You can get one thousand no's, but it only takes one yes to take your idea from a concept to reality. It may take weeks, months, or years, in spite of that you have to be willing to tough it out. Ride your idea until the wheels fall off. Don't expect anyone to believe in you if you don't believe in yourself. The time to build up your faith and courage isn't while you're in a battle. Faith muscles are mainly built overtime with daily preparation for the day war comes knocking on your door. When fear, doubt, fatigue, and their allies show up, you're already in fight mode. There's no need to get ready when you're already ready.

The greater the challenge, the greater your Inner-G will shine. Battles, enemies, and challenges are not placed into your life to weaken you. They are put before you to make you stronger, and more durable. You'll notice that fear and fatigue are just optical illusions, smoke and mirrors, to place doubt into you.

Laugh a Little More. A Lot More

Would you believe me if I told you children laugh 200 times a day, while adults only smile and laugh an average of four times a day?[33] As adults, we're fortunate to have stress in our lives. Believe it or not, some stress is good for us due to the fact that it helps motivate us to get off our butts and to do something about the situation. But remember to have fun. All work and no play creates a very uptight individual. This is why vacations of some sort are extremely necessary so that you can laugh in a relaxed state of mind, and not tensed up all the time.

---

[33] Gerloff, Pamela. "You're Not Laughing Enough, and That's No Joke. Psychology Today." Jun 21, 2011 https://www.psychologytoday.com/us/blog/the-possibility-paradigm/201106/youre-not-laughing-enough-and-thats-no-joke

Living uptight and on edge, all the time wears down our body and impacts multiple aspects of our lives. A stringent life causes a lack of energy, digestive problems, and poor decision-making. Laughter is a natural medicine that rejuvenates our spirit. In a sense, laughing out loud moisturizes our mind, similar to what lotion does to our skin. Think of all the bone-dry people walking around, moping about their day. It's actually healthy for you to laugh since your quality of life may very well depend on it.

"A happy heart is a good medicine and a cheerful mind works healing, but a broken spirit dries up the bones."
PROVERBS 17:22

Instead of crying at adversity, laugh at it. Crack a smile. Wink your eye. You have nothing to lose and everything to gain. Do something positive in opposition to the current situation. One of the benefits of laughing is the reduction in blood pressure since laughter triggers the right side of the brain and releases a natural tranquilizer that relaxes us during those edgy, stressful times. And the cherry on top is that laughing actually helps us get rid of depression and improves our sleep; it's the difference between sleeping on a pillow made of feathers or concrete bricks. Some people, unfortunately, depend on drugs, excessive sexual activities, or if they're smart, utilize exercise to deal with stress. There is a plethora of self-destructive behaviors people take part in to deal with the weight on their shoulders, but laughter is literally the best medicine.

Watching the evening news will make it quite challenging to laugh. Here's a good tip for you: Stop watching the news every day! You have a choice to stop or reduce most of the negative things that try to enter your ear and eye gates daily. Feeding your supercomputer heinous crimes against children, murders, corruption, and the unemployment rate won't make you laugh. At least I hope not. It may sound strange but tune into a cartoon or a good comedy movie every once in a while. It helps make the heart lighter. Make sure it makes you laugh your heart out. You'll feel the tension begin to ooze out of your body, while both your attitude and imagination will improve.

Which Side of the Brain Do You Use the Most?

The Left or Right.

Left Brain	Right Brain
Thinking in Words	Visualization
Sequencing	Imagination
Linear Thinking	Intuition
Mathematics	Rhythm
Facts	Holistic Thinking
Logic	Arts
Reading	Adventurous
Analytical	Daydreaming
Reality Based	Using Feelings

Laughing stimulates many organs of the body, especially the brain, where you may feel it tingling with excitement—a brain tickle. It enhances your intake of oxygen-rich air stimulates your heart, lungs, and muscles, and increases the endorphins that are released by your brain, which sends dopamine in to provide a sense of pleasure, reward, and happiness. That, in turn, simultaneously makes the immune system work better and changes your brain wave activity to what's called a "gamma frequency," which amps up your memory and the ability to recall things easier; in other words, it makes you smarter. Now, how do you like them apples?

According to the Law of Reciprocity, applying the power of smiling means the universe will smile back at you. The reason successful marriages continue to thrive isn't that they read Bible quotes together, had the best love-making sessions, or because they went out to eat every weekend. The fire in their relationships continued in order to keep their hearts smiling towards each other by cracking knee-snapping jokes, spending quality time together, keeping their complaints to a minimum and compliments to a maximum, and laughed more than they argued. The same goes for many of the world's greatest athletes and warriors on the battlefields. When they found themselves under immense pressure, they smiled or laughed at their challenges. We see it all the time. One of the greatest athletes to ever grace the track was a smiling sprinter named Usain Bolt from Jamaica.

Usain has won an astonishing eight Olympic gold medals and eleven world titles under his belt. His trademark became starting and finishing his races with the biggest smile on his face. He's usually the only track athlete laughing on the starter blocks, while the majority of the sprinters were all tensed up or sweating buckets. These runners don't even smile for the cameras, mainly due to the fact that they are "in the zone". Over time I realized he was laughing to relax meanwhile gleaming with confidence in his mind that the race was already his. And guess who would win nine out of ten times? He has maintained the record for the fastest time in both the 100-meter dash (9.58), with a top speed of 27.8 mph, and the 200-meter dash (19.19) to date in track and field history.[34] As a retired athlete of the sport, it was inconceivable that anyone could run that fast—it seems superhuman. There's a very good chance we won't see his records beat until the year 3022. The point here is that he smiled all the way to and through the finish line.

---

[34] World Athletics. "Olympic Games Records." https://www.worldathletics.org/records/by-category/olympic-games-records

"Winning isn't everything but wanting to win is."
VINCENT THOMAS "VINCE" LOMBARDI

Just like the Bolts of the world, we need to smile our way to and through the finish lines of our lives. Through the storms, the difficulties, heartaches, and the darkest hours until you find the silver lining. There's always a light at the end of the tunnel. You just have to keep pushing until you get there, no matter what. No retreat, no surrender. As long as you don't expect to move as fast as Wilma Rudolph, Jesse Owens, Usain Bolt, or Florence Griffith Joyner overnight, you'll be A-OK!

To be a winner, you have to be able to see yourself as a champion, act like a champion. Master your craft with class. Learn as much detail as possible about your goals so that your elevator pitch will be two-thumbs up quality. Own your craft from conception to manifestation. Claim it. Put your name on it! There is no way you can accomplish this with a piss-poor self-image or half effort. It's mandatory to erase the failed self-image that you've been fed and continue to work on improving your character. Each of us has the right to drink from our lake of abundance, live freely, and happily. Turn that losing picture of yourself into a loving, successful self-image. Anyone trying to steal your joy, light, destiny, or smile is the enemy. Point blank, period! Many of us make the mistake of thinking that we have no enemies, therefore we don't perceive that there's anything to protect. Just because you don't have a problem with someone doesn't mean that they don't have a problem with you.

The present time is a good time to start repeating the following daily:

"Wow, I always look good, but today, I am exceptionally fine! I am rich beyond measure. I am rich in good health. I am rich with bank accounts filled with money. I am rich with love because I choose to be."

Final Thoughts

The ideas that you have about yourself will determine how far you go. Tear off those negative labels handed to you. Fight back by turning the curse of the Double F's around and with a cheerful smile as you speak words of affirmation to the universe daily. Replace condescending thoughts and words with positive ones, "I am prosperous and successful!" and in the words of the late great Muhammad Ali, "Look how beautiful I am!"

Recognize. Activate. Create. Reel in your dreams by practicing the necessary actions associated with them as if what you prayed for is already here.

DREAM POWER: THINGS TO REMEMBER

- Dreams often contain signs of the future.
- Write down your dreams when you WAKE UP and while it's still fresh.
- Dreams create desires, which lead to greater expectations from you.
- We are equipped with willpower, hope, vision, and imagination.
- Visualize your desired future frequently.
- Courage and faith will destroy fear and fatigue every time.

8

STOP MAKING EXCUSES—MAKE IT HAPPEN

AVE YOU EVER WOKEN UP AND JUST DIDN'T HAVE the drive to get out of bed? It wasn't because you were sick or in pain but because you didn't want to deal with the problems waiting for you on a silver platter. We all have days like these, from the richest to the poorest. The key is to shut them up! Silence those thoughts of doubt and defeat as soon as they enter your mind, otherwise, they'll direct you into a trap; diverting your attention away from where it needs to be. We have to guide our inner conversations by the way we communicate with ourselves. What we say to ourselves will either motivate or deter us. Remember, your words must have the correct corresponding action. In this case, after you tell yourself to shut up with the complaining—pray, clap yourself happy, get up, wash up, and get going with having a marvelous day.

When you think and speak negative thoughts about people, situations, and undesirable outcomes, you'll repeat those toxic ideas throughout the day and may even wake up with those same thoughts on your mind the next day. We'll literally concentrate ourselves out of position to receive the blessings and opportunities we worked so hard for. Think of it this way: Instead of talking yourself out of pursuing your dreams— reverse the curse. It's asinine to be your own dream killer. Talk yourself right back into your aspirations!

Depression is usually the result of unchecked negative inner conversations overpowering your positive ones. The only failures in life are those who never tried. The only losers are those who never attempted to win from within. Repetition is good for comprehension purposes, and I can't say this enough: It's mandatory to get rid of the defeated self-image. You'll be fighting an uphill battle if you don't. People seldomly win uphill battles.

Many of us know of someone or quite a few people who make as many excuses as there are leaves on a tree. It's a habit that becomes dangerously part of their identity, consciousness, and reputation; having a good reputation is power in itself. One definite sign that you aren't living your best life is when you barely have control of your time and space, jumping to other people's beat (employer, ex-husband/wife, landlord, or etc.). That isn't power—it's called being a puppet. You cannot win under this condition. While this may be true, that doesn't mean you don't fight to change the dynamics of power towards your favor.

In truth, I always wondered why many of my friends and family members had to wait until the last minute to do almost any and everything; even when it was for their own benefit, while others never missed a beat; they were on top of things like white on rice and flies on...well, you know the rest. On top of that, they always seemed in control of their time, making all the right moves that were fruitful and prosperous. This proves that my theory of progress was correct. In order to be successful, one has to consistently make good decisions for their future. At the same time, to be unsuccessful one either doesn't put forth their best efforts or consistently makes unwise decisions.

In addition, when something crosses our mind that needs to be done, especially if it's important and time-sensitive, we must will ourselves to jump to it and get it done. It behooves you to implement this advice if you know that you can be slightly lazy at times or just a flat-out couch potato. Deciding not to decide is a decision in itself that can have undesirable consequences. Getting things done early is better than completing them late. I used to think being early was for nerds and the corny types. To be honest, arriving early shows that you have power and respect the time of others. It also gives us enough time to think, be relaxed, and calm before important business meetings, (romantic) dates, and job interviews. Being punctual allows our swag extra time to warm up and fully captivate those we meet instead of feeling rushed, sweaty, and offbeat. Early is being on time, and it leaves a great impression. Waiting until it's almost time to head to your meeting is too risky. God forbid you get stuck in traffic due to an accident on your way to a meeting or job interview, those few extra minutes could cost you dearly. It's foolish to purposely add extra pressure to yourself when you're already under duress. Some stress is great to have but too much will cause you to fail what you're trying to accomplish and lose your mind in the process.

For instance, if you have a 1 pm interview, and it normally takes 30 minutes to get to your destination, leave your home at 12 pm instead of 12:30 pm. In fact, leave your home at 11:50 pm, just in case, with a good book to read, while you practice and wait. A friend of mine lost a $110,000 salaried technical consulting engineer position that was already in the bag. She was fifteen minutes late to her third and final interview with the company, which was to officially accept the position. She underestimated the downtown Atlanta mid-day traffic, and it cost her big time. It took her over a year and dozens of interviews before finding another job, but nothing was ever close to that six-figure salary or status. Ouch! Her experience gave me the wisdom to be early, and not on time. It is better to be safe than sorry.

At times, we may procrastinate because we perceive the task at hand to be too difficult or somewhat painful. One thing about pain is that it's inevitable, but misery is a choice. Denzel Washington, a two-time Academy Award and three-time Golden Globe Award-winning actor, once said, "The greatest threat to progress is ease. There would be no Cicely Tyson, Viola Davis, Taraji P. Henson, Chadwick Boseman…or Denzel Washington if it were easy." Progress can and will be painful, so prepare your mind for it. Look at it this way: Discomfort comes with the territory when you're reaching for new heights. Growing pains are great signs of progress. You don't have to live in the pain of the past or be afraid of the distant future. By no means am I saying you should ignore what or who caused you a great deal of suffering, but you do not want to acknowledge the hurt more than you acknowledge your joy of living today? Directing too much attention away from your dream gives those who crossed you the power to do so again. Where your attention goes, your power flows. Stop giving irrelevant people power over you and start harnessing your own.

PROCRASTINATION CURE

Successful people recognize when they're procrastinating and quickly shake it off because they're wired to be industrious 24/7. Overachievers don't know how to turn off their ambition. The problem lies when you don't recognize your lackadaisical spirit, which is actually a curse. We've all dragged our feet in one form or another. It's important to figure out the reasons for your delaying tactics so that you can eradicate that lazy spirit. Some people find certain tasks or jobs aimed toward attaining a goal unpleasant, and that becomes the source of their avoidance.

FOUR INSTANT ANTI-PROCRASTINATION STRATEGIES THAT WORKS!

- ➲ **Have clearly prioritized to-do lists,** schedules, and time frames for completing a task, and lifelines for goals to help counter procrastination.
- ➲ **Work backward from your lifelines** (~~deadlines~~) to know how long you need and when to get started so you're not late.
- ➲ **Do it today!** Why put off until tomorrow what you should do today. You'll be able to relax your mind once you've accomplished your task(s).
- ➲ **Focus on one task at a time.** Contrary to popular belief, multi-tasking is often counterproductive. There's a myth out there that being successful means acting with warp-speed urgency and doing as many things as possible at the same time. Actually, the most successful people are very patient and avoid juggling many tasks due to the chances of making errors increase by 50 percent. In fact, neuroscience research shows that multitasking is not the best way to get things done, and it can be damaging to our brains. On top of that, we make more mistakes, and it zaps our energy over time.[35] Yikes!
- ➲ Finally, like all well-organized people, **make sure your work is broken down into manageable steps.** This helps you avoid taking on more than you can chew.

The legendary Olympic champion Wilma Glodean Rudolph came out of the womb having to jump over life's hurdles with excruciating pain. Wilma could've easily given up as a child due to her handicap. Unfortunately, many of our precious children have given up in unimaginable ways to cope with the stress that generations before never had to deal with, such as cruel bullies in school and online, let's not forget

---

[35] Dr. Napier, K. Nancy, "The Myth of Multitasking." May 12, 2014. https://www.psychologytoday.com/us/blog/creativity-without-borders/201405/the-myth-multit

to mention the social media depression. They aren't equipped with the consciousness to protect themselves, which is why parents have to take the time to step in as support to defend their children, build up their confidence with positive affirmations, and teach them about their history to enable their self-discovery.

Born prematurely in 1940, one of Wilma's legs was shorter than the other. Stricken with double pneumonia, scarlet fever, and the poliovirus at the age of four gave her left leg and foot problems which caused her to wear a large, uncomfortable brace. To make matters worse, her feet became twisted until she was nine, and by that time, her doctors told her she would never walk again. Her queen mother, Blanche Rudolph, heard those words and, like any great parent, stepped in and spoke the exact opposite to her daughter. "My doctors told me I would never walk again. My mother told me I would. I believed my mother." said Wilma.

She chose to believe in her mother's words and her God-given abilities over the negative reports of the doctors and the naysayers. In the same way, as a sunflower leaning towards the sun, her mind, body, and spirit tuned in to what her mother spoke over her as a child. Wilma's faith was fully engaged and was ready to fly. She overcame insurmountable disabilities and became a phenomenal athlete, competing in the 1956 summer Olympic Games. There was no room to be lazy. Being a black woman and an athlete during the Jim Crow era, you have to applaud and respect her mammoth-sized commitment and dedication to her craft. In Berlin during the 1960 Games, she became the first American woman in history to win three gold medals in track and field at a single Olympics. The cherry on top was that it was also the year the Olympic Games were televised for the first time which made her an instant international celebrity. In her mind, she was already a superstar long before the world caught up to her bright light. Her radiant smile and humbleness matched her talents. Wilma Rudolf was out of this world!

"Winning is great, sure, but if you are really going to do something in life, the secret is learning how to lose. Nobody goes undefeated all the time. If you can pick up after a crushing defeat and go on to win again, you are going to be a champion someday."

WILMA RUDOLPH

Wilma Rudolf showing off her 3 Olympic gold medals

WHEN IT COMES TO YOUR
DREAMS MAKE NO EXCUSES

Stevie Wonder and Ray Charles were both blind yet became two of the best musicians and performers in history, with millions of record sales, and 39 Grammy Awards between them. Nola Ochs graduated college at ninety-five years old. Ronnie Lott, former defensive back for the San Francisco 49ers, played with a broken pinky finger and decided to have it amputated so he could play right away. On April 1, 1976, Steve Jobs was on the verge of going broke when he founded Apple, Inc., now one of the largest mobile phone and computer companies in the world, with his partner Steve Wozniak.

Another prime example of a highly spirited winner is the American-born in 1906, Josephine Baker, who became a world-renowned French dancer. She grew up in the slums of East St. Louis, one of the worst ghettos in America during the early 1900s. There were times that she had to search through garbage cans for food to bring home to her family to eat. However, that didn't derail her dreams since Josephine's eyes were locked on the stars above and not on the slums below. When life seems low it's better to look up high and into the sky. At only 19 years old she packed up and boldly moved to Paris, France when the opportunity came knocking in 1925. She was hoping for a miracle so badly that if a hint of an opportunity came whispering at her door, she would've jumped to it. Her friends were skeptical about her decision to leave the country, but to Josephine, anything was better than going with the flow and allowing complacency to eat away her destiny. She took France by storm and they loved her. All of Europe adored her. Josephine was the equivalent of what Beyoncé is today.

One of my favorite entrepreneurs was previously mentioned in the introduction, Mr. A.G. Gaston, aka The Black Titan. I loved the little I heard about him so much that I read his autobiography twice, maybe even three times, entitled, The Black Titan: A.G. Gaston, the Making of a Black American Millionaire. His story starts on July 4, 1892, in Demopolis, Alabama. He honorably served in the US Army while in France during World War I, but he couldn't find respect or work in the United States like most black men and women during those dark days. Mr. Arthur George Gaston was fortunate enough to find work in the coal mines of Alabama at the Tennessee Coal, Iron, and Railroad Company.

"Save a part of all you earn. Pay yourself first. Take it off the top, and bank it. You'll be surprised how fast the money builds up. If you have two or three thousand dollars in the bank, sooner or later somebody will come along and show you how to double it. Money doesn't spoil. Keep it."

A.G. GASTON, *GREEN POWER*[36]

It was while working at the coal mine that he realized that most of the men there were bachelors, both white and black, and didn't have lunch to eat while on their break. Mr. Gaston immediately saw green! His hundred-million-dollar empire began with bringing extra sandwiches for the fellas and they bought them like hotcakes. From there he started loaning them money at 25 percent interest. The mining business has always been a dangerous enterprise, but even more so back in the early 1900s since the federal government did not have laws in place. The miners barely had any safety measures, no savings, no health or life insurance, if they died. Black widowers had no respectable place to bury their husbands, due to the Jim Crow laws, forcing people to bury the deceased wherever they could with dignity. The mining widows were forced to ask (sometimes beg) for donations at the mines and local churches. Mr. Gaston saw another opportunity and started the Booker T. Washington Burial Insurance Company in 1923.

He would later purchase a property to create a funeral home to give the black community a respectable place to bury their loved ones, hence the birth of Smith & Gaston Funeral Home. From there he opened up a training facility to teach black folks how to work in the insurance and funeral industries with his second wife in 1939, Minnie L. Gardener Gaston, who was already a teacher; his first wife, Creola Smith Gaston, passed away in 1938. Minnie's experience as an educator and the love they had for each other was

---

[36] Gaston, A.G. *"Green Power: The Successful Way of A.G. Gaston." Big City Brands, LLC.* 2013

perfect for his vision. When they opened the doors to their school, hundreds of eager black students drove in from all over the country. White colleges wouldn't accept them, so they went to one of the only places that welcomed them at the time. Tuskegee University was another option in the same state. Now, get this—there were so many students on opening day that the Gastons were joyfully overwhelmed. They were forced to purchase another property nearby that same day in order to have room for them. Money talks loud and clear.

1939, Students and Staff In front of the Booker
T. Washington Business School

*"**Stay in your own class.** Never run around with people you can't compete with. In other words, let the Joneses do what they do. You don't have to keep up."*

MR. GASTON'S MEMOIR, *GREEN POWER*,
10 RULES FOR SUCCESS

Mr. Gaston, being the opportunist, knew all too well that black people couldn't book a hotel room in Alabama. He took it upon himself to also be the first African-American to purchase and own a motel chain. This was critical because when Martin Luther King, Jr. and other civil rights activists came to town they didn't have to drive all night looking for a clean place to shower and rest; they no longer had to sleep and eat in their cars. The A.G. Gaston Motel was in the center of the Birmingham Civil Rights movement. In fact, Mr. Gaston also secretly sponsored the bailing out of the Civil Rights leaders from jail. He didn't want the authorities knowing that he was the big timer bankrolling their freedom. His net worth was more than $130,000,000 at the time of his death on January 19, 1996. I can go on and on about Mr. Gaston, but I don't want to spoil the fun. You'll just have to read about him yourself. He inspired me to become the entrepreneur that I am today. His empire started with selling one sandwich and a handful of peanuts, so don't despise humble beginnings.

Last but certainly not least, Jack Ma is another entrepreneur extraordinaire that I'd like to share with you due to his humble beginnings and astonishing rise to the top of the world. He grew up dirt poor in Hangzhou, Southeastern China, and couldn't afford to drag his feet, especially if he was going to avoid the guaranteed fate of poverty surrounding him. After years of hard work, Jack saved enough to earn his way to America, only to be turned down numerous times by fast-food jobs, including KFC. He couldn't catch a break if he paid for it, including when it came to the colleges he applied to. Harvard University turned him down ten times, but he remained <u>committed to his vision</u> of making it big somehow, someway in America. He ended up finding work as an English teacher, getting paid a minuscule amount a month and was determined to remain persistent in pursuing his dream.

For the first time, at the age of 31, he used the internet and became optimistic in regard to the potential of doing business online. He saved up enough to invest in a couple of online businesses, and the third one was the jackpot: a company called Alibaba Group. He was able to convince seventeen friends to cram into his little apartment to listen to his vision and invest $60,000 into his dream. In 1999, the idea was an e-commerce company that would connect Chinese merchants with foreign markets, allowing exporters to post their product listings so that customers could buy in bulk directly from the site. It was a brilliant idea! It was such a success that the entire economy of China substantially increased. "Alibaba facilitated 80% of China's e-commerce, 60% of all parcel deliveries, and $170 billion in total transactions—more than Amazon and eBay combined."[37] Jack was the blessing that the e-commerce world was wishing for. He took internet shopping to a whole new level.

Fifteen years later, Alibaba became one of the most valuable technology companies in the world after raising $25 billion, the largest initial public offering in the U.S. financial history. Jack Ma is not only the second-richest man in all of Asia (4.7 billion people) with a net worth of a measly $42 billion greenbacks. Those friends that invested in him are now all multi-millionaires. It pays to really support your friends beyond likes on social media. Jack Ma was named as one of Asia's 2019 Heroes of Philanthropy for his work supporting underprivileged communities in China, Africa, Australia, and the Middle East. Again, I say, never despise humble beginnings. Way to go, Jack!

---

[37] Levin, Ben. "How Alibaba Became More Valuable Than Facebook." Newsy.com, September 19, 2014. https://www.newsy.com/stories/how-did-alibaba-become-more-valuable-than-facebook/

Final Thoughts

Everyone mentioned was handpicked since they all had a rough start in life. Some of them were blind, handicapped, oppressed, or born into poverty. One common denominator between them is that they all made it happen. As captains of their fate they took life by the horns and stirred it towards the direction of their destiny. Life is too short to not to give it your all-time best. Triumph cannot be obtained without the struggle.

STOP MAKING EXCUSES. MAKE IT HAPPEN!

9

TIME AND SPACE
IS EVERYTHING

*A*N OLD STRATEGY OF WAR THAT IS STILL USED today is to get your enemy to exert energy into meaningless battles so when it's time for the decisive war, they'll be too tired to fight. Ultimately, they'll be forced to surrender and wave the white flag. The trick is to learn to pick your battles, so you'll have the mental strength and physical energy when it's most needed. How much time and energy have you squandered because you've allowed a petty situation to take control of you instead of taking control of the situation? You are a winner, not a loser. Start by stop losing time. Stop losing your focus if you expect to win. Take ownership of the spirit of the winner that you are. You have to know that every battle isn't worth fighting. Every argument that presents itself isn't worth your attention. In fact, most of them aren't worth a fraction of your oh-so-precious time, but they're so easy to get pulled into like a whirlpool. Once you're in it, you'll find yourself asking, "How did I get in this mess?"

The victory starts in the mind. You'll have to see the "V" in your head prior to seeing it in reality. It's not difficult to do once you've given yourself permission to be second to none. For those who may find it challenging to take on the spirit of a winner, the solution is easy: time travel. We travel back and forth in time all of our lives through a plethora of methods that include music, folklore, food, movies, cars, intimate kisses, and our tattoos to name a few. In doing so we bring back old memories of joy, and many times pain. Let's choose food, for example. Some dishes have been handed down our family line for generations; resurrecting the heartwarming feelings of Sunday's family dinner that has been a family tradition for ages. Once we eat a scrumptious meal that reminds us of eating with our family, we think about those memorable times that we sat together.

What if I were to tell you that books carry time sequences, as well. Intentional reading can also be uplifting if you know what to look for within the black ink on the pages. Find someone in recent or ancient history that inspires you enough to study their interests and dislikes by investigating their stories. Their stories are literally, treasure chests filled with a wealth of knowledge that can change the trajectory of your life, on the condition that you take heed to their wisdom by applying their steps to success. Reading isn't just fundamental, it can very well be a joyful experience as you dive into the author's powerful world of words, energy, and everything in between. It's the building block to discovering your gems of rich history, self-identity, and brain tickles.

Reading The FACTS of Life:

Did you know that the predicted number of future prisoners is calculated based on the children's third-grade reading levels within the U.S.? The U.S. prison planners use their local third grade reading scores to predict our future behavior, and how many inmates they can count on to fill the new prisons.

Data shows that illiterate third-grade children are four times less likely to graduate than students who can read by that age, which leads to dropping out of school. High school dropouts are three times more likely to be imprisoned than those that graduated. In Texas, for example, uses fourth-grade reading scores to project how many prison cells they're going to need for the next 10 years. The prison-industrial complex is fueled by the $5 billion dollar yearly average that private correctional facilities have been making since 2015.[38] It is unfortunate that the government would rather spend $47,000 a year to keep a young man or woman imprisoned instead of spending $10 for a children's book. This is why it is vitally important to invest in crime prevention programs, such as our Rosette Pierre's Creative Arts Center, which is geared towards helping children from urban communities to read and explore different careers in the various forms of art. We're helping them reach their highest potential in order to avoid the school-to-prison pipeline. Similar programs don't line up the pockets of the powers that be therefore they aren't financially supported on the level necessary in order to be successful.

Therefore, it's clearly up to us, the community leaders with the love and resources, to fund these critical educational programs for our youth. There is an ongoing war to destroy our children's future before they even have a chance to establish their self-awareness and purpose.

A.G. Gaston's Black Titan biography written by his granddaughters is a perfect example of a story that's worth looking into. His $130,000,000 kingdom started by selling sandwiches, popcorns, and

[38] White, C. Martha, "Locked-in Profits: The U.S. Prison Industry, By The Numbers." NBC News. November 15, 2015. https://www.nbcnews.com/business/business-news/locked-in-profits-u-s-prison-industry-numbers-n455976

peanuts. Your billion-dollar empire may start by selling lollipops. There may be an interview or video recording from a documentary that you can watch to solidify what you've read on a particular person. You'll notice a transition taking place when you're transported to their time and space, in their shoes so to speak. Biographies are the next best option, but there is nothing like hearing it from the horse's mouth. Can I get an Amen? You'll learn new lessons that are meant to improve your life. The Honorable Marcus Mosiah Garvey, an extremely successful businessman in the 1920s, once said my favorite quote of all time:

> "If you have no confidence in self, you are twice defeated in the race of life. With confidence, you have won even before you have started!"[39]

Please allow Mr. Garvey's profound quote to marinate in your spirit for a couple of minutes before continuing to read. My interpretation of this quote is that you're defeated in two ways, spiritually and in reality, when you don't have confidence in yourself or your God-given abilities. Furthermore, in the latter part of the quote, I believe the Honorable Marcus Garvey was saying, with confidence, you've spoken to the universe and received the victory in your spirit first, therefore anything that you place your mind towards with great intensity must manifest. You can't lose with God and the universe on your side. Everything happens in the spiritual realm before it manifests in the physical realm, your reality. That is why it is vitally important to not waste time pondering whether or not you'll be victorious in the fires of life ahead. You're giving yourself a fighting chance to win when you speak and think positively. Remember, **Positive In, Positive Out!**

---

[39] Garvey, Marcus. "Marcus Garvey Life and Lessons: A Centennial Companion to the Marcus Garvey and Universal Negro Improvement," University of California Press. 1987.

It all starts and ends in the mind, so only dwell on the good things that you desire to have and to be. It may take years to accomplish your dream but remember this when it seems like it will never happen: A dream delayed is not a dream denied!

The God you are praying to is inside of you right now and has always been. You are a god. You and I both have the power to create. It's up to us to reach God-consciousness, also known as the highest level of spiritual awareness. It has the capability of pushing you to reach a higher level of manifestation and inner peace. The body will grow old and die off, but the spirit is infinite and lives on. Having God-consciousness enables you to pray and tap into the secret messages and signals that The Creator and the universe is channeling your way; it also allows you to make fewer mistakes and a plethora of brilliant decisions.

"My only distinguishing quality is that I didn't quit."
NIPSEY HUSSLE

With a clear mind, we usually figure out the right decision in retrospect of the wrong choice. Those ill-advised choices sometimes cost us our valuable friendships, irreplaceable time, homes, large sums of money, and unfortunately, even our very lives. Wouldn't it be great to make the right decisions by knowing that the end results will be in your favor? Having God-consciousness empowers you to know the end from the beginning. In time, you will cease praying for what you already have. Instead, while praying you will thank our Creator in advance for the victory. And by the way… praying can be done in silence anywhere, such as on the beach under the bright sun or the shiny stars. It doesn't always have to be in the darkness of your bedrooms with the door shut. You'll begin to give God thanks before the business deal is done; before you've received the college acceptance letter; before the baby is born; before you close on your new home. You'll joyfully speak to your future, "It's already looking better for me!" We speak to our past all the time, and for what? It makes perfect sense to fall in love with your future because tomorrow never looked so good! Everything is getting better for you.

God-consciousness allows you to take action with the right attitude, even in the midst of life's storms. Instead of timid, "bummer prayers" telling God, "I'm not worthy," with your mind fixated on things like hairdos, the latest smartphone, or rent money. You'll be praying boldly, claiming your peace and prosperity. In your prayers you'll be paying off mortgages for others that are in need since you will have more than enough to give and to invest in others who are serious about accomplishing their dreams. Blessed to be a blessing! Everything can change for the better at any moment. You are a shiny star getting ready to receive blessings coming from the north, east, west, and south.

We all know that there is more power to the giver than the borrower. The borrower will be entitled to the lender until the debt is paid. No one with self-respect wants owing anyone on their conscience, especially when the other person is conniving. There was a time when people would be enslaved until they worked off an outstanding debt. And if the father didn't pay the creditor, then his wife and children will pick up the tab, continuing where he left off.

It's a completely different mindset when you change your thought process in a positive direction. And if you wish that direction to be in finances, your lifestyle will take a Cinderella spin going from consumer to producer. Concede in your mind that the power of God's divine knowledge is in you. Utilizing your mind power gives you the strength to be done with failure, mediocracy, and anything holding you down from elevating to a higher dimension of success. I said it once, and I'll say it again. As long as you don't quit—you are bound to succeed! You are a success! You must believe that about yourself. Knowledge is power, and the lack of it leads to destruction. You are loved and have the DNA of The Creator within you; therefore, you can create the good life you want and deserve. While you're wishing for a miracle, don't forget the miracle you are. Knowing that you are special is a power within itself.

"Put your name on your miracle. Claim it!"
REVEREND IKE LEGACY

Do me a solid. We're going to do some magic together. Point your finger at yourself and say the following incantations:

> *I am so gorgeous. My mind is beautiful. My divine self is extraordinary. My divine self is prosperous. My divine self is successful. I rejoice because of it. It's getting goodier and goodier today, tomorrow, and forever.*

Yes, you've read it correctly. Goodier is a notch better than good! The Creator gave you the vision to write that book. You were given the responsibility to start that business. You were given the vision to purchase that big house on the hill since the majority of your life has been plagued with instability. You were given the resources to open up a boarding house for broken people to help them become whole again. It wasn't given to me—it was given to you, and only you can give birth to it.

"If God can get the blessings through you, then God will get the blessings to you!"
PROPHETESS YVETTE BRINSON

Don't Stop Believing

A variety of things aren't and will never be in your control, however many things are. You can't control the clock, but you can determine what you do with every minute, but only if you're conscious of the time. You can't direct the weather, but you can aim to weather every storm that comes with life. You can't prevent accidents from happening to you and your loved ones, but you can control how you maintain your peace. You can't control other people's road rage, but you have the power to not engage in verbal attacks or throw the bird back at them (fight the temptation).

You have control of what you dwell upon, and equally, as important, you must have complete sovereignty over your faith! You can have faith the size of a mustard seed or the size of a skyscraper, but it's the action with your faith that matters. See your goals manifesting before they do. Why not dwell upon getting that raise at your job or that new business grant for your youth museum you've been keeping your fingers crossed for? What you put your mind to is what you create. You have to receive it in your mind and spirit with the feelings of excitement to bless your vision. Your feelings are what you water your seeds of faith with. It's the feelings that get the blessings. The question is where are you planting your seeds?

Life was designed for us to advance, increase, and love others while we share the air above the ground; it wasn't designed for us to stand still and be angry until we die. Although I must admit, fate does have a way of making us doubt ourselves with all of its firestorms. But when that happens, remember that it is written,

"Greater is he that is in me than he who is in the world."
1 JOHN 4:4

Reminding myself of this fact helps tremendously whenever I'm faced with insurmountable adversity; knowing that "I AM" activates my divine inner powers and attitude from zero to one hundred real quick, similar to when Clark Kent switches into Superman in the telephone booth. Mind over matter is using your willpower to overcome physical obstacles. Some look at them as problems, while others, with the proper disposition, view them as opportunities to shine.

One of the best modern examples of someone who never stopped believing in themselves was Steve Jobs. He revolutionized both home computers and smartphones. Globally, over 4.8 billion people are carrying mobile "smart" phones, which is hurting our intelligence, but that's a different story. Steve made plenty of mistakes when creating the first Mac computer, yet he wasn't afraid to carry on. As a leader in technology, he quietly worked out the kinks until he perfected his craft. His critics didn't believe that he was qualified since he never graduated from college and only finished about six months of education in 1972 at Reed College, a small school in Oregon. He dropped out because he felt college tuition was too expensive for his parents. Steve had to sleep on friends' floors and couches when his pockets were low. There were times when he would walk miles to get free meals from the Hare Krishna temple. He remained hopeful even though it seemed like he failed in life until he was informed about a calligraphy class that was being offered. It was time spent wisely in this class because it planted the seeds for him to create his first Mac computer that eventually revolutionized the computer industry. And over time, he would go on to create the iPod, iPhone, iMac, MacBook, and iPad. At the time of his passing, Steve Job's net worth was only $10.2 billion, and he was a member of Disney's board of directors, but that position was only paying him a measly $242 million a year.

"My favorite things in life don't cost any money. It's really clear that the most precious resource we all have is time."

STEVE JOBS

There is going to be a time when all of your physical efforts and money won't be enough. This is the time when you're going to have to dig deeper than you've ever dug before. You're going to have to go harder than you ever thought or imagined possible. When you've used up all of your strength, this is when your Inner-G kicks into overdrive, the supernatural power of The Creator steps in to give you favor during your darkest hour; both your enemies and fears will be devoured. When you are pursuing your dreams with all of your heart and soul, there arises a greater power from within to accomplish them. Oprah Winfrey said it best, "I believe that every single event in life that happens is an opportunity to choose love over fear."

One of the many things I love the most about eagles is that instead of flying far away from the storms, they fly towards them. They find it fun and challenging, while all of the other animals and people are panicking while doing their best to get as far away as possible. Eagles have a great time in the storms, soaring through the air without even having to flap their wings as if they're windsurfers catching a wave. It's breathtaking! Could you imagine having fun while facing life's storms head-on? You'll have your loved ones and critics bamboozled! I'm sure, as a trailblazer, Steve Jobs experienced this firsthand.

Steve Jobs Holding The iMac At MacWorld 2007

People will think you're crazy, and you'll be labeled as the one that flew over the cuckoo's nest. Well, I have news for you. If you're going to go crazy, be crazy with ambition towards a positive direction. Become possessed with the thought of winning your race in life to the point that there's no way you can lose. People thought I was too young and had a few loose screws at the age of thirty-two to write an autobiography as my first book. People criticized my relationship goals book, *7 Types of Queens, King's Desire* since I wasn't married yet. However, I was invited to be part of an international book tour in London. People shunned my first two films (a short film and a documentary), which both did well. But when the finished product was completed, many of those same critiques became customers and top supporters. I didn't wait for the storms to go away, nor did I wait on the support of those I was one hundred percent sure would have my back. I kept my praises up, stuck to my script, and constantly spoke my desires into existence, even when I had to convince myself to keep believing that I would be successful.

As you know, life will throw many curveballs at you. People will approach you sideways, so be prepared to happily swing your bat at adversity. Pause the champagne popping until you see your victory all the way through, until your vision has come to pass. Many of us celebrate too early, only to have our plans sabotaged because we announced it too soon and the right people with the wrong intentions took notice. Knock on wood. First and foremost, hold your horses and will in the victory with everything you've got — mind, body, and spirit!

Remember, it doesn't matter what it looks like or what others think about you. The only opinions you should be concerned with, in most cases, are yours and those who show you love. You got this!

Don't tell anybody this top-secret information, but the secret sauce to my success comes from repeating this acronym:

S.

B.

E.

Say this after me:

SPEAK IT. BELIEVE IT. EXECUTE THE PLAN.

Speak your goals repeatably. Positive incantations are influential due to the simple fact that they remain on our brains, motivating us to take the necessary actions towards accomplishing our goals. Speak your dreams loud and proud. Speak them so the universe hears you loud and clear. Speak them so that your ears can taste your dreams as they seep into your soul and flow throughout your body. Speak them until your ancestor's spirits wake up to applaud you. Speak them until you've brought them into existence one step at a time.

Decree and declare your goals. Below are quick and simple affirmations that you can speak over your life:

*"I am more than a conqueror, no weapon formed against
me shall prosper. I will get this new job! Thank you for the
promotion! I will close on this house any day now! My health
is getting better."*

Allow me to rewind a little bit. Did you catch that? "I *will* get
that promotion!" "Thank you, God, for the promotion!" The latter is
speaking from a future position and not wishing but feeling that you've
already obtained it. Become your own fortune teller. As we visualize our
dreams, we're bringing the future into the present. Foresee the feelings
of joy and excitement you'll feel by sharing the good news of <u>giving
yourself that promotion</u> that you've been waiting for as if it has already
happened. The present you're living in is the future you've created in
the past based on a collection of thoughts and the choices you've made
to secure it.

Increase Your Brain Power with Feng Shui & Healing Crystals

Healing crystals are great for decorations, but they do much
more than brighten up a room. Crystals absorb negative energy
and emit positivity. Healing crystals magnify your energy to
manifest your thoughts, including peace and abundance on
all levels. This is why the popularity of crystals, such as jade
and quartz, dates back to ancient times. They bring positive
energy and promote self-sufficiency. With every deep, conscious breath you hold with the jade stone in your hands, you
can exhale all the worries and pains that are holding you back
from your natural state of joy. Jade gives you the wisdom to
see past self-imposed limitations and helps shed that outdated,
can't-win-so-don't-try attitude. It's believed that the power of

crystals wasn't just for jewelry and regal decorations; they were used to alter the weight of heavy objects such as three-ton stones in Kemet that were utilized to construct gigantic pyramids and incredibly large statues of pharaohs.[40]

Incorporate a jade crystal into your daily meditation to lift the pressures of life weighing down on your shoulders; have the courage to discover your divine inner truth while discarding any negative patterns holding you back from your full potential. Jump-start your meditation practice with the lush and verdant shades of jade, the good luck crystal that brings abundance and prosperity into your life. While all crystals promote harmony between the mind, body, and spirit, the Jade crystal is a super-star in the world of crystal healing, thanks to its green connection to the heart chakra.

In addition, ancient civilizations once considered jade as the most precious and naturally beautiful material. In China, by 3,000 BC, the jade crystal became known as "yu" or the "royal gem." It was carved as early as the Neolithic period (c. 3500–2000 BCE) when it was mainly used as jewelry for royalty, who were revered as divine. The precious gemstones were also used to make sacrificial and ritual objects, especially in the Hongshan and Liangzhu cultures.[41] In feng shui, jade has been used for centuries due to its ability to create a serene feeling of inner harmony and balance.[42] Jade is also used as protection and good luck. You can find endless good luck charms made of jade for various purposes, from creating wealth to attracting more friends.

In addition, jade jewelry is also a popular feng shui application for body energy, which is just as important as your

[40] Dr. Llaila Afrika. "African Holistic Health." New York City. A&B Publishers Group, 2004
[41] Sessums, Zoë, "7 Simple Ways to Use Feng Shui in Your Home." March 14, 2020. https://www.architecturaldigest.com/story/simple-ways-to-use-feng-shui-in-your-home
[42] Anjie Cho, Anjie. "The Basic Principles of Feng Shui." May, 14, 2020. https://www.thespruce.com/what-is-feng-shui-1275060

home's aura. One obvious meaning of the jade stone is purity or purification. And because jade is regarded as a stone that protects and supports heart energy, it also symbolizes gentleness, nourishment, good luck, protection, and prosperity. Also, adding in decorating elements of metal brings the qualities of sharpness, precision, and efficiency into your home or office. Its balanced presence will help you live with clarity, the sharpness of thought, and calming, balanced energies. All of the above equates to increasing your productivity.

There are goals in life that we may feel we're not well equipped to go after. Degrading thoughts beget more of the same. Maybe you're feeling how I used to feel: "I'm not good enough. I'm from the hood. I have a criminal record and bad credit. People like me don't go to college and start fabulous careers. We go to prison or die early in the streets." This is exactly what crossed my mind hundreds of times when I stepped back on the college campus. You're not qualified as long as you keep saying that you're not. You are what you think you are. But if somehow you can muster up the reserves to see yourself in a positive light, then you are great enough! Like so many others that seen the light, I went from the 'ghetto to get-mo' because I desired to.

Over time, I realized that if I were to defeat the odds and succeed that I would have to discover the secrets from the trailblazers before me. Therefore, I began to study remarkable individuals that escaped their war-torn environments. For example, former President of Burkina Faso, Captain Thomas Sankara (Thomas Isidore Noël Sankara), and Percy Miller, aka Master P, both gentlemen were able to become highly successful despite the odds stacked against them. What was their secret? And more importantly, how can we get our hands on their green print so we can follow suit?

Let's begin with Master P, born and raised in New Orleans' Fifth Ward Calliope Projects, one of America's most violent ghettos. He was brought up with sixteen people in a three-bedroom apartment. If you've ever watched any of the documentaries about the impoverished neighborhoods of New Orleans, it's hard to believe America has cities that look like a third-world country—a flat-out war zone. It was so dangerous that children at the age of five had to have life insurance policies due to the madness of stray bullets flying around as if it were *Star Wars*. The death of his brother, Kevin Miller, really inspired him to be as successful as possible to move his family to a safer environment with his record label No Limit Records. Master P went from pain to purpose.

While most young men in his shoes would've blown their $10,000 inheritance in one weekend in the club, towards car rims, or on a shopping spree, he turned his small fortune into a half-billion-dollar empire. He helped create several millionaires within his sphere of influence, including close family and loyal friends. He had the mindset already in place, and once he received a little capital, he wisely sought advice from Michael Jackson's attorney for $25,000, which lead him to negotiate one of the largest deals in the entertainment industry.

Instead of getting one to three dollars per record sold, he was able to broker a distribution deal with a major record label by obtaining 85 percent of the sales plus 100 percent ownership of all master recordings. This was an unprecedented business deal! Obtaining 100 percent of your masters is unheard of in the music industry since that is where all the real money and power are found. Whoever owns the masters owns the rights to the song. Keep in mind that after years of saving from his out-of-the-trunk CD hustle and music store sales, he came to the negotiating table to strike a deal with $250,000 of his own money to pay for the marketing of his music. Now, he has a net worth of over $250 million and counting. He's become a rap mogul, entrepreneur, former NBA player, sports agent, filmmaker, and most importantly to him, a philanthropist who is giving back to inner-city youth and the elderly.[43] He mastered his craft to become one of the wealthiest entertainers of our time. If he could miraculously make it out of a warzone and do well for himself, then why not us? We can and we will!

"Even when I was in the ghetto, I was saying that my mindset was different: 'I live in a mansion.' I was always that little kid thinking I'm in a mansion even though I was in poverty. <u>I never said I was broke.</u> I've always said, 'The money is in the mail; it's coming.' Just the power of words. And I named myself 'Master P' because I wanted to master whatever I do."

Furthermore, as Master P elevated financially, he lifted those that were with him and supported his vision. Likewise, President Thomas Sankara, at the young age of 33, raised up the consciousness of an entire nation by first stripping his country's inherited name, Upper Volta, from French colonial power in 1984. Captain Sankara renamed it with an uplifting title, the Democratic and Popular Republic of Burkina Faso, which means "the land of upright men" or "the land of the incorruptible people." Yes, the name came with a new flag and national anthem, as well. It makes perfect sense to go all the way through with a complete makeover to cut out all of the cancer that the past oppression left on the minds and spirits of the people. This one chess move gave the small West African country a huge sense of pride and honor to build upon, and Burkinabe worked enthusiastically to live up to it.

A mental transformation took place from being poor and begging for aid to becoming rich in selflove—working and doing for self. There is no better feeling than independence and to have complete sovereignty over your livelihood. [It's very important to take note here how the power of names, labels, and titles encourages levelheaded people to do their best. It gives people a prize to keep their eyes on and a reason to lift their heads up.] Renaming the country was a prophetic move within

---

[43] Wagner, Betsy, "How Master P Turned $10,000 Into A $250 Million Fortune," July 19, 2019. https://ca.finance.yahoo.com/news/how-master-p-turned-10000-into-a-250-million-for-tune-201641409.html

itself for there is history and energy with every name. President Sankara left a profound legacy of success on multiple levels in a very short amount of time. His blueprint must be thoroughly studied and replicated today in all countries that are struggling to maintain a self-sufficient economy, thriving health and educational system.

President Sankara became an international figure for refusing foreign aid from the enticing International Monetary Fund trap. Being the young and charismatic leader that he was, noticed how history showed that countries who accepted funds from the IMF or foreign countries were often enslaved economically with debts that could never be repaid; amongst many issues, this gives the lending country the ability to find an excuse to go to war, take over, or even place a trade embargo that can choke the economy of defaulting nations. He said, "I believe that the poor and exploited do not have an obligation to repay money to the rich and exploiting.[44]

Instead the president reduced the reliance on foreign aid by boosting domestic revenues. In other words, everything that Burkina Faso wore, ate, and drove were made in Burkina Faso. With this strategy he was able to get one of the "poorest" countries in the world out of debt in three years. He forced every village to build a medical dispensary and had pharmacies built in 5,384 out of 7,500 villages. Once he stepped into the presidential office the first priorities in his *written plan* were feeding, housing, and giving medical care to his people who needed it desperately. This was a formidable task that would take a clear plan, and the entire country to toss their hats in—all hands on deck! The infant mortality rate dropped from 208 per 1,000 births to 145; the infant mortality was about 20.8%, during his presidency it fell to an impressive 14.5%. His administration was also the first African government to publicly recognize that the AIDS epidemic as a major threat to all of Africa.

But that's not all. The children benefited too. School attendance under Captain Sankara increased from 6% to a staggering 22%. He also

---

[44] Thomas Sankara: The Upright Man. California Newsreel. http://newsreel.org/video/thomas-sankara-the-upright-man

understood that the status of women in any country is a reflection of the wealth of that country. He took it upon himself to elevate a large number of women into top positions in government, including the army, an unprecedented policy. He wanted to encourage them to work outside of the home, since the brilliance of women and their divine feminine energy was too powerful and resourceful to be kept solely on domestic work. President Thomas Sankara was the first president in world history to boast that he was a feminist. He was truly loved by his people, and only God knows what else he could've been able to accomplish if given more time and space in the world. He was the president from 1983 to 1987.

Take advantage of the time and space to embrace the special moments and celebrate those victories. Do your best to celebrate people within your circle. Don't be selfish, for they have victories that are worth making a big deal over too. A true winner understands the sacrifice of others and the level of commitment it takes to obtain significant accomplishments.

Every little victory should be acknowledged and celebrated. In due time, your self-value and confidence will increase. With enough victories under your belt, you may begin to get the 'big head', which is fine as long as you're able to remain humble. For it is better to have over-the-top confidence than to have no faith yourself. A celebration doesn't have to be grandiose all the time. It could be doing something simple as buying yourself a delicious sub, reading your favorite book, watching your favorite childhood movie, or cooking a scrumptious meal. With that being said, make a big deal out of everything you've been triumphant in. Whether it's removing debt off of your credit, regaining a lost friendship, saving money you would've otherwise lost, or getting a good grade on a hard test.

In addition, buy yourself the most expensive ice cream in the store, and share that moment with someone you know who will be happier for you than you are. Celebrating others while the momentum is high is easy. Once the momentum is gone, the time to ride that wave of energy will be gone as well. Honoring them when the excitement is low shows that you've got the heart of a champion because victors encourage other victors. In his book, *The Art of War*, Tzu Su, an ancient Chinese warrior, emphasized that it's an advantage to have the natural elements of Mother Nature and time on your side during a battle than to be against them. That's two less foes that you'll have to face and two more allies that are actually working on your side. For example, do your best not to fight uphill battles if you can avoid them. It takes a lot more effort to fight upward and a lot less to fight an enemy going down a hill. This makes perfect sense according to the Laws of Gravity. It's easier to walk down five flights of stairs than it is to walk up them, correct? It takes less energy, and the momentum pushes you down. True friends are here as natural allies to push us up when the momentum is low during those uphill battles.

Final Thoughts

You must recognize that controlling your time and space is vital to your existence. It's the difference between simply living or thriving. Use the natural elements of Mother Nature and your circle of influence to boost your positive energy. Celebrate your victories and learn from your losses. The latter is so much sweeter and has better options.

5 EASY WAYS TO UTILIZE YOUR TIME AND SPACE

- ➲ Cherish your time and space as if it were diamonds. You determine its value.
- ➲ Control what you can control in your life. Don't sweat the small stuff.
- ➲ Time travel to someone's time by reading their inspiring story.
- ➲ God-consciousness allows you to take action with the right attitude, even in the midst of the storms.
- ➲ Practice the art of Feng Shui in your living space. Start small by adding a plant, a healing crystal, or a beautiful painting.

10

PROMOTE YOURSELF

*I*N LIFE AND THROUGHOUT HISTORY, THERE'S PRO-gression and regression. History proves that people, civilizations, and cultures, in general, don't naturally progress in their advancement in a given society just because. Regression takes place all the time, in fact, some civilizations have regressed to the point of extinction. With the support of the community, individuals within the culture will have to advance in order for the entire culture to survive in our ever-changing world. There is a level of fulfillment when you're able to promote yourself at will rather than waiting for a supervisor, or mythological deity on a purple unicorn to hand it over on a silver platter. Entrepreneurs thrive on making things happen. They go into each meeting knowing that this might be the big payday. One day your finances will catch up with your valiant efforts to make your mark in the world. "The Money Is Coming!"

There is nothing like being independent calling your own shots. Once you've reached the wealth accumulation stage both wisdom and humbleness will guide you on how to be a true blessing to your community, and not just figuratively. One sad mistake we make is thinking that progress happens overnight or is guaranteed overtime. This is clearly not the case. Progress happens for those who make the conscious decision to achieve it; the victorious are those that are determined and refuse to give up!

As a baby, we don't automatically start to crawl, walk, and talk. Children have to will themselves to advance in life. They have to fight a hundred times a day to get back up after tumbling and stumbling. If there's a will, there's definitely going to be a way! It's funny to watch, but I believe these precious little gifts take our laughter as an encouragement to keep trying; some cry, while others laugh, but they keep trying their best to walk and promote themselves. With a smile, they keep trying over and over again until, one day, they begin to take that first step. A momma eagle will push her chicks that are afraid to try and fly out of the nest after three months. It may sound harsh, but either the chicks fly or they end up as ant food. Friends, in the same way, you'll have to find your wings; push yourself to learn something new that will improve your quality of life.

"A thousand-mile journey begins with one step."
LAO TZU

Key Ingredients For Self-Promotion

1) A Vision
2) The determination of a lioness
3) A positive self-perception
4) The fighting spirit of a lion
5) Controllable environment

As mature adults, we have to will our hearts' desires toward what we want out of life. The Bible says, "Faith is the substance of things hoped for and the evidence of things unseen." The "unseen" part is the unknown, invisible spiritual realm. This is where all the true power and miracles take flight. If you can see it from within, you can do it. All you're missing is a little courage to believe in yourself, faith in action, and to be prepared for the opportunity. When that time comes around for you to shine, you'll be ready with the right attitude of gratitude—the sky is the limit. It's absolutely amazing what you can do when you have confidence in yourself. Without a shadow of a doubt, if there is a will, there is a way to make it happen, especially when all hope seems to be lost.

Never stop improving yourself, expanding your knowledge, and acquiring new skills. According to the billionaire business tycoon Warren Buffett, "Investing in yourself is the best thing you can do. Anything that improves your own talents." He adds, "If you've got talent, and you've maximized your talent, you've got a tremendous asset that can return ten-fold." In other words, keep investing in yourself, own your talents, and you'll reap the rewards. But hey, what does he know? He's only worth somewhere around $83 billion.

The same confidence we once possessed as a child and teenager has diminished over time due to the reality bug bites that we've received. The realization that we can't just wake up and magically become a doctor, an astronaut, a teacher, a preacher, a restaurant owner, or a lawyer vanishes. For starters, we have to go to school for a set number of years, study and do whatever it takes to hang in there long enough to receive our degree and eventually obtain our dream position. Hopefully, the student loans aren't too high that you can't enjoy the fruits of your career that you've worked so hard to achieve.

The time and space in between reaching the zenith of your career as an entrepreneur, or whatever profession you choose, won't be a piece of rum cake. It will consist of battling lions, tigers, bears, and dragons, which are represented by slumlords, the injustice system, gatekeepers, in-laws, tornados, attorneys, robbers, foul co-workers, and crazy exes. And let's not forget you may have to walk on fire (hopefully this won't be needed but you never know). The victory over each of these pressures will shape and define your confidence. The good news is—you don't have to do it alone. Great friends will help you toward your goal and they'll see it as their purpose to assist you. The Creator already has guardian angels waiting to support you along the way to help you fulfill your purpose. Your actions will be the guiding light that will draw them to you. There is a caveat, however. You must use discernment to determine whether or not each individual that enters your life is a true ally or an enemy spy keeping tabs on you.

Climbing over your first mountain is always the hardest. Evolving as an author wasn't easy, especially with my first book. The first hundred pages were handwritten in a notebook since I didn't own a computer or desk up to that point. My fifth-grade teacher, Mrs. Sonji Wyche, whose been teaching for over 30 years, since 1990, taught me how to improvise when it came to handling my business, eradicating excuses all together. She was a phenomenal leader, very stern but fair and loving. Mrs. Wyche knew how to challenge her students without verbally hurting them, which ultimately created a student army of overachievers. My classmates were all blessed by having the honor of being her first class of students after she retired from the U.S. Army.

While growing up our desk was the dinner and living room tables, or a book on our lap. Thanks to Mrs. Wyche's advice, when our lights were cut off, we stood by our window to catch the streetlight in order to complete our homework. Moving along, I was 25 years old when a drug addict sold me his old desktop computer; I had to utilize the floor and typed until my neck and arms were hurting. I found encouragement in the compelling feeling in my gut to write since I've experienced so much adversity. My soul had to be put down on paper in hopes that others will be empowered to prosper as well. The reality is that I was able to overcome the stigmas and traps of my environment, the ghetto, plus the criminal justice system by not going with the flow. By the grace of God, I found a way to graduate college. I then went on to hold top positions within corporate America which wasn't a small feat at all and is why I felt that my story needed to be recorded. The world needed to hear my story as an encouragement. If I can rise above my situation, so can you!

People told me I was too young to write an autobiography. I was also told that I'd never get a publishing deal, graduate from college, or be wealthy. But you know what? I chose to ignore the naysayers and promoted myself knowing that I was already wealthy spiritually. Had I selected to listen to their doubts I would've never seen myself as someone great going somewhere greater. I smiled at them just like a child and kept on fighting, refusing to give up, refusing to be denied what I knew that I deserved deep down in my heart and soul. I proved them all wrong, and the financially wealth part will come any day now. The money is on the way! Get those doubters the heavens out from your immediate environment. Their unbelief and lack of faith will not only minimize your power and potential, but they'll also ruin your dreams. In fact, they are Dream Killers (DKs). When they see you, they'll say, "Here comes that dreamer!" The more you speak about your vision the more they'll despise you. Point out who the DKs are and strategically remove them from your circle on your terms but do it expeditiously. If you wait for them to depart, they'll leave after they've flushed your dreams and valuable time down the toilet. Act now, not later. It's only your livelihood at stake.

Furthermore, I didn't just give myself promotions in life. I created my promotions! Being Mr. or Mrs. Nice Guy isn't going to cut it in this dog-eat-dog world. You won't be running through the sunflower field wearing a straw hat and kissing the clouds. Sometimes you have to be assertive and stake your claim. Take life by the horns and stir it the way you want instead of following the latest trends. In many instances, the right choice isn't the most popular one. People who unfailingly "go with the flow" all their lives are really scared of taking control. Many of them are simply conditioned to only do what they are told. The wind can blow every which way, so going with the flow, without fail, is the worst way to go about achieving your goals. I started my own marketing company and made myself president; from there I started my own publishing company and gave myself a publishing deal.

When the recession hit in 2008, and many companies shut down causing a disastrous domino effect in the real estate market. My years of experience running a marketing company gave me the leverage I needed on my resume to get my foot in the door in corporate America. Companies were impressed and gave me the salaries I demanded. Promoting myself was a matter of survival. Why? Because I knew my worth as much as they did. There was no way that I was going to settle for a $50,000 yearly salary knowing that my experience qualified for $90,000. Now, how do you like that? Everything we want has been given to us already. You just have to claim it by putting your name on it, working your dream into existence, and speaking it until you see the manifestation. Sam Cooke said it best, "I'm going to sing, and I'm going to make a lot of money!"

When you look at social media, there are tons of people doing amazing things but why are they really on these platforms? There are film producers, attorneys, mothers, fathers, authors, singers, actresses, actors, teachers, community activists, pastors, YouTube scholars, parents, dancers, internet historians, relationship/life coaches, church groups, and vegans—you name it! What do they all have in common? Most of them are seeking recognition and support from strangers for their greatness, while others are campaigning to earn your business. You may get lucky and go viral causing your website sales to go through the roof overnight, but that's like winning the lotto. The sad part is that most of us are seeking affirmation, and recognition for our greatness from people who will never pitch in a dollar towards our vision, not one red penny. They wouldn't support you even if they lived across the street from where your event was being hosted. Trust me, I've been there. A lot of that has to do with their self-hatred, which breeds envy because you've got the guts to after your dreams and they don't. Who gives a

Gilligan's Island what non-supporters think? It doesn't make sense, but it's the reality of the world we live in.

In the biblical story of Joseph, he didn't have time to ask his siblings why they didn't love him or why they refused to recognize his special talents. He had to deal with the reality of being sold into slavery by his own family, being set up for a crime he didn't commit, and then being thrown into prison, indefinitely. Even then, his talents could not be silenced. He improved his solid character and talents while he was in the dungeon, a dark place, which led the way for him to meet the pharaoh and become the second most powerful person in all of Kemet. The rest is history! Joseph had the perfect response to a time and space that would've been soul-crushing to anybody. It is said that your talents will make room for you at the table of kings and queens.

All the recognition in the world doesn't mean a thing if you don't recognize your own magnificence. Wealth only amplifies who you already are. Here's the kicker: Greatness has nothing to do with how good-looking you are, and neither does having millions of followers and likes online. People that think so have a false sense of reality and need to snap out of it. Having lots of money doesn't make any of us a better person either. Greatness has nothing to do with the bankrolls of cash people flash all over the internet and in the clubs. Prominence has everything to do with how many people you lift up and have a positive impact on. How many families have you saved from tragedy, such as stopping them from being kicked out of their homes and into the streets? Shaquille O'Neal, retired NBA Hall of Famer, once moved an Orlando family from living on the streets to an apartment. Great people do great things! Booker T. Washington, my favorite educator of all time once said in his monumental book *Up from Slavery*, "Those who are happiest are those who do the most for others."

Spectacular Reflection

In serving others, we find the significance of our lives. I can guarantee you that you won't find your purpose through selfies. Through servitude is where we're able to locate our true greatness, and how you'll find that *spectacular reflection* in the eyes of others. When light hits an object, three things can happen: The light reflects off the object, the light goes through the object, or the light is absorbed by it. The same applies to people. Your light represents your energy. The brighter your light is the higher your energy becomes. The darker your light becomes the more depressing and boring life will be. Your light will bounce off of some people, while others will absorb it. Your positive vibrations will illuminate the faces of the people around you with a smile. When you connect with the right people, they'll believe in you and will be on the same wavelength, your light will reflect theirs, and vice versa.

Mr. Self-Promotion himself, Tyler Perry, doesn't need an introduction. His story is incredible. It's amazing that he went from being abused as a child by his father, to living on the streets, and somehow kept writing his scripts. He eventually had a street and interstate exit signs in Georgia named after him which is nothing short of remarkable. Tyler is the epitome of self-advancement and self-promotion. When he first started producing his plays, barely anyone would come, but he didn't allow his discouragement to override his vision. He penned his way to the top by building his own studio where he produces his TV shows, blockbuster movies, stage plays, and music.

As a result, he went from having nothing more than a plan, a dream, and determination. He then consistently worked his faith into action to become one of the most prominent figures in all of Hollywood. All things considered, he consistently stuck with writing his film scripts to become a wealthy actor, producer, director, writer, playwright, author, songwriter, and now a wealthy real estate developer. Mr. Perry also purchased 330 acres of land in Atlanta at the former U.S. Fort McPherson Army base for the low price of just $30 million. Wow! As of 2019, Tyler Perry Studios is the largest film production studio in the United States, and it officially makes Mr. Perry the first African American to outright own a major film production studio. He is a living legend that has climbed his way up to work with the top names in every aspect of the entertainment industry.

After all, to promote yourself, there is one simple first step that can't be ignored: Stop demoting yourself! Tear off the negative labels that have been spoken over you. The labels of regret, abuse, poverty, and lack. Peel them off one at a time by writing, speaking, acting, and thinking the opposite. Peel off poverty and replace that label with one of financial wealth, riches, and glory. See yourself in your garage, finding it difficult to decide on which car to drive within your fleet of Rolls-Royces, Range Rovers, and Ferraris. Rip off the label of sickness and replace it with one of good health, wholeness, and happiness. See yourself stretching your legs and arms on a tropical beach with the sun rays smooching on your sun-kissed skin, having fun working out in a gym. Can you see yourself jogging in a beautiful park with the leaves falling and the sound of water flowing in the creek? With every step you take, each leaf that falls on you represents a new blessing you are walking into. It's already looking better for you!

You have the power to empower and promote yourself, so use it. It's the only way you'll see your spectacular reflection inside of you that's anxious to be set free from the darkness of isolation and the clouds of doubt. CAGED EAGLES CAN'T FLY. Don't allow yourself to be like Baeksul. Let your inner greatness soar!

ATTITUDE DETERMINES ALTITUDE

Pay attention to your chi, the balance of Yin and Yang; the positive and negative electromagnetic energy that flows through everything in creation. There are multiple aspects in the world that aren't in your control, yet it is within your authority to make adjustments to the energy around your humble abode that will increase your peace of mind. In time, you will see the benefits of positioning your mind in a calm place so you can think clearly, even amongst the most dangerous and toxic surroundings. Many of us are forced to live in an abusive, violent, and noisy environment that seems inescapable, however, let's not forget that it is only temporary, for it is written by you. You are one day closer to having the good that you wish to have and to become the person you desire to be. History gives us plenty of examples of incredible individuals that defeated the odds —on the condition that you truly desire to, you'll be next.

Now, since most of our immediate environment is within our power to alter, take advantage of the ability to do so, today. This is where the ancient Asian practice of feng shui comes in, which involves intentionally balancing the energies around your home and place of business with the positioning of furniture, colors (colorology), creative art, plants, natural wood, metal, and healing crystals; all of which can be purchased at a thrift store, garage, or estate sale for dirt cheap. The beauty of it all is that you can practice feng shui on a shoestring budget, and it makes you look rich; it's so serenely powerful that it resonates with all cultures and won't impede on your spiritual beliefs. You can ball out on a budget, and be at peace.

With this in mind, what is colorology, and how could it be used to improve my daily life? Colorology, also known as chromotherapy, is a type of therapy that allows color to "balance" emotional, physical, spiritual, or cognitive "energy" an individual may lack."[45] According to

---

[45] Yousuf, A. & Raza, S., A critical analysis of chromotherapy and its scientific evolution. Evidence-Based Complementary and Alternative Medicine. (2005). 2(4), 481-488. http://www.trconnections. com/Colorology_Brochure.pdf

research "chromotherapy provides colors to the electromagnetic body or the aura around the body, which in turn transfers energy to the physical body (energy field that can be captured by Kirlian photography discussed in Chapter 7). This makes chromotherapy a form of therapy... a system of treatment that can benefit people because of its harmonic relationship with nature. Everything that exists in this world is a combination of different colors. Colorology also suggests that colors have multiple healing effects, and certain colors can invoke a variety of responses from cognitive, emotional, social, spiritual, and physical changes.[46]

To demonstrate, match your surroundings to the frequencies of the thoughts you want to call forth. Let's say that you want to be a world-renowned author, it behooves you to surround yourself with book on perfecting your writing and books by other renowned authors. The frequencies of our thoughts are described as the meaning of colors, also known as the "aura." For example, let's use blue since it's one of my favorite and most used colors. If you think about relaxing your mind with blue surroundings, it will amplify your thought process. Note that when you step out of your home in the morning and the sky is perfectly blue, your heart and mind instantly feel relaxed before you have time to think about anything else. This is because any thought in the direction of relaxing the brain is assisted by the heavenly blue vibration of the sky. When the sky is gray, you may begin to have depressing thoughts before you even realize it. That's how fast the mind picks up on colors, symbols, shapes, and words. The brain picks up on things faster than we can snap our fingers. This is why it's critical to clear our mind on a regular basis, by dumping the unnecessary images and thoughts.

Different shades, tints, and hues of blue have different meanings. Dark blue can be seen as elegant, rich, sophisticated, intelligent, and old-fashioned, while royal blue can represent superiority, and light

---

[46] The Meanings of Colors: Symbolism, Color Therapy and Psychological Effects of Colors." Psychologia. https://psychologia.co/meaning-of-colors/

blue can mean honesty and trustworthiness. Notice how the blue-ribbon represents royalty and first place. The creation of the color royal blue came from a competition to make a dress for Queen Sophie Charlotte of England. The queen was the second Black Queen of England (Philippa of Hainault was the first) when she married George III of England on September 8, 1761. The royal couple must've had an awesome marriage because the two had fifteen children together.[47]

Blue is considered to be the calming color of water, and the heavens, dominion of the gods. People are more productive, for some reason, in blue rooms. In fact, research shows colors can improve one's reading ability and comprehension, particularly for those with learning disabilities. Other colored overlays show benefits when it comes to reading skills, but the blue overlays show a significant increase in improving reading skills in all types of students.[48]

In addition, high culture civilizations have utilized colorology for healing for centuries. Chromotherapy was used in Kemet and Ancient China. For instance, red was deemed to stimulate the body and mind, which is why they wore red coral beads and crystal jewelry, such as red rubies and red corals, wherever they could be seen on any given individual. Red can also symbolize love, enthusiasm, fire, life force energy of blood, chaos, destruction, action, and protection. Pink symbolizes confidence, passion, fun, and love. Orange symbolizes energy, warmth, and socialization.

Green is the symbol of nature, vegetation, new life, growth, and good health; it improves vision and is easy on the eyes. Interestingly enough, for those that are into Kemetic science, green was the color of the "Eye of Horus," or *Wedjat*," which had healing and protective powers, therefore the vibrant color also represented well-being. Doing "green things" was to have a positive behavior in life-affirming manner,

[47] African American Registry, "England's Black Queen, Sophie Charlotte born." https://aaregistry.org/story/englands-first-black-queen-sophie-charlotte-born/
[48] "The Link Between Color and Reading Comprehension" K5 Chalkbox https://www.k5chalkbox.com/color-and-reading-comprehension.html

such as "going green". Today, the green movement has picked up a lot of momentum over the years by promoting the recycling of products that can be reused. Our collective effort helps reduce the consumption of our resources, eliminate unnecessary wastes, to conserve natural resources and forests, reduce pollution, which is very positive towards our overall health, and to increase the longevity of our planet for the next generation.

For those with a website, it's highly suggested you utilize a money green "Buy Now" button. It's an inviting color. Watch your clicks and sales increase. It may seem as if you're manipulating your online visitors. Well, not quite, so don't feel guilty. You're encouraging them to make purchases that they want to make in the first place. Notice how bright and colorful most department and tech stores are.

Everything is energy and has a certain vibration. Stones and crystals enhance our energy sources. The colors of waterfalls, creeks, and mountains make people feel really good, which is why those areas were always considered prime real estate. Since the beginning of time, civilizations have built their villages, temples, and castles around flowing water. Building a home around these tranquil geographical features and color schemes has been known to help individuals feel better and relaxed. When you feel better, you think, act, and sleep better, right? And with that, you're able to make superb and strategic power moves that leads to a stable, peaceful, and secure livelihood.

When waking up in the morning, you should feel blessed to see the sunrise in all of its glory, acknowledge that you've been given another chance, and the opportunity to live your best life. Even if you wake up to the thundering rain, greet the day as if it's raining blessings upon you and your loved ones. With this type of revelation and can-do attitude, how could anyone not be excited about life? Whether it's raining, sunny, or snowing, tell the world, "It's going to be a lovely day!"

Some of the best greetings are, "It's a great day to be alive!" and "I'm blessed and highly favored!" Speaking those types of good wishes carries the high vibration necessary to remain positive and spiritually high. All of which adds up to a very attractive personality. With so many gloomy thoughts, salty people, and detrimental events trying to keep our spirits down on a daily basis, we need as many positive thinking strategies as possible to combat them. When you're having disempowering thoughts, shift them with thoughts that empower you, such as divinity, love, volunteering, and etc. Refer back to your M.A.P. (Must Achieve Purpose) for inspiration.

When feeling down and out—it helps to think ourselves happy. Better yet, clap to yourself until you're feeling better. Give yourself a round of applause! It will change your down-and-out mood into a more uplifting one. Motions give us emotions. A lot of people don't move around enough causing their life to be boring, rigid, and mundane. Yuck! Clapping to yourself is a mood-altering activity that knocks the dust off your spirit and the rust off of your body. It will motivate you to MOVE into feeling better about yourself, and your situation, even when it appears there is nothing to clap about. Allow your words of affirmation to be the impetus to push you forward with a confident pep in your step.

Our words carry a different level of energy and can possibly change someone's mind from committing suicide or from making an awful decision. A gracious attitude has the power to bless others and makes our relationships all the more pleasant to be in. You may be the only god a person may ever come across. Without the right energy, your relationship is bound to fail, unfortunately. No one wants to be in a serious relationship or married to someone that is malcontent, they will zap the love, life, and energy right out of you. Life will greet you the way you greet it. It's the Law of Reciprocity and Attraction in action. A great attitude attracts great people to your well-lit life like moths to a flame.

Your attitude determines your altitude. A good attitude helps you find your life's purpose easier, as you continue to walk toward reaching your destiny. You can reach a higher elevation and can see better with a light heart and not be held down with the darkness of hatred, anger, and the heavy weight of regrets. That's not living! Having the correct reaction to life's situations gives us the chance to be optimistic, and if you have high hopes, it carries you to another dimension of possibilities. Do you want to fly high or continue to crawl while pecking at the ground until you bump into your miracle? Bishop TD Jakes once said in a sermon that people hang around those who feed their egos because they thrive on that attention.

However, these types of people will deplete your resources, such as enthusiasm, energy, food, and money. Too many of us are hanging around people who need us due to the void that's in their lives. That's not necessarily a problem as long as they are contributing back into your well of light, but the wrong types of people will ruin your positive attitude. How is that? A person with a bad inclination doesn't have the spark to maintain or jump-start someone's depressive state of mind with positive vibes. More than likely resentment between the two of you will build up if it hasn't done so already. No one has time for that.

People, pets and even plants have energy emitting from them. Everything breathing projects energy into the atmosphere. People will drain your positive energy if you allow them to continue speaking negative thoughts around you, or by constantly pulling you away from your life's work in order to entertain their selfish needs. Ultimately, you'll be derailed from promoting yourself, and will ultimately, you'll be demoted from your very purpose. I've lost count of how many bright futures I've seen robbed from individuals by the circle of friends they hung around. Birds of a feather flock together since they're familiar with each other and operate on the same wavelength. There's a saying, "Show me your network, and I'll show you your future." Those with high positive attitudes repel from those with a foul one mainly due to the fact it's hard to communicate with one another; they'll always clash over the simple things since it would be impossible to see eye to eye. Our perspectives have a lot to do with our environment (home, workspace, and neighborhood) since it controls a high percentage of our mental state's "peace of mind".

The classic Skinner Box Experiments with rats were produced by Dr. Burrhus Frederic Skinner, a psychologist, and author. His experiments proved that we are our environment considering that where we live and how we live determines our actions and behaviors. Dr. Skinner placed rats into his famous Skinner Box (he invented) to show how positive reinforcements, such as food and water, or negative reinforcements represented by electrical shock would influence the rat's behavior. The rats quickly learned to stay away from the lever that delivered the undesirable outcome of the electrical shock.[49] The point here is to do all you can to avoid the negative souls and situations that are causing you grief and pain. It's hard to be positive when everything around you revolves around negative reinforcements: poverty, sickness, negativity, violence, and destruction. Even if you don't currently have the financial means to relocate, it doesn't cost a thing to free yourself mentally. All it will cost is for you to pay attention—analyze your environment and make the necessary changes that you can control. In due time, with the right grind, you'll be able to live where you can be at peace. It's no wonder hoarders can't think straight owing to the fact they're surrounded by filth from the floor to the ceiling. Bless yourself for a change. You deserve it!

Let's take a moment to talk about how this affects children. It's amazing how something as simple as a new pair of shoes alters our attitude. We can go from feeling okay to feeling fantastic! It makes us excited about stepping out, and it cultivates a new positive attitude and self-image. Especially, when you're used to wearing dirty shoes. Children who aren't emotionally strong and confident become easily depressed when they don't have a new pair of shoes on the first day of

---

[49] Theodore, "Skinner's Box Experiment," Practical Psychology: https://practicalpie.com/skinners-box-experiment/

school while the other students are showing off their new kicks; to add insult to injury they're usually picked on and bullied. Therefore, parents must build up their children's conscious rather than material gratification. It's when a person places too much value on material things that they are prepared to fatally wound others in order to maintain possession of them. It's vitally important to teach your children that they control their destiny by working smart and hard towards what they want to accomplish, not by what name brand is trending.

Wisdom entails surrounding yourself with people who can take a load off of your shoulders with wise counsel. And since you are a woman or man of honor, you're going to return the favor by taking a load off their shoulders. You don't want to be caught in a foxhole or on a battlefield to find out the person you risked your life to save won't shoot a single shot or tell you to hit the deck to save yours in return. This may sound like a cliché, but it's true that some people are in your life for a season, a reason, or for life. Be sure to keep the bond close with the lifers since you'll continue to be a blessing to one another, similar to how a great wife is to her awesome husband, and vice versa. One hand washes the other, and both hands clean the face.

A Golden Cage Is Still A Cage.

A horrible attitude holds us back from so many opportunities. Terrible attitudes force people not to want to be associated with you, and it scares people from approaching you even when it comes to business. Now, unless they are your family members, and even then, they'll say, "That's just the way she or he is," even though they'll barely accept your buffoonery out of loyalty. Foul attitudes block the blessings from reaching us. It also tends to make the years longer since it takes a lot more energy to be mean than it is to be nice to people. A negative can't-do-it attitude literally cages you from your full potential. No matter how much money or fame one has —a golden cage draped in diamonds is still a cage. Imagine being wealthy and kind—you'll be a one in million type of person! Those who have developed a lifestyle around their cantankerous orientation will find it difficult to shed that mindset, but it's not impossible. Some people have been negative for so long that they don't realize it or care to work towards changing that part of their character. Unless, by some miracle, someone they love begs them to try and be nice. It will take serious consistent effort to get out of your "life as usual" disposition. In reality, you'll have to really want to improve.

Statistics show that attitudes make a significant difference in the health of our mind and body.[50] A positive attitude makes it easier to accomplish your goals, keep friends, build stronger marriages, and maintain good business relationships. People with a positive attitude tend to get sick less than the average person, and in many cases, when they do get sick, they get well faster. Positive thinking helps with stress management and can improve your quality of life and health.

As I came into my life's purpose at the age of thirty-two, I put my foot down and said to myself, "You're almost forty. Tighten up and go harder!" I had an epiphany to get away from just feeling great about myself and instead do a lot better in helping others; to make volunteering a weekly occurrence, rather than just on the few traditional holidays. You never know when it's going to be your last day on earth. If I were to die today, I would be satisfied with the amount of service I've done through my community efforts alone. Giving to others has a way of elevating your self-worth and uplifting your spirit. Helping others is the best part of the self-promotion process. Closed hands can't receive blessings. The acts of charity are one of the most powerful actions of love that accelerates the undertaking of healing our broken wings. Hanging

[50] Mayo Clinic Staff. "Positive thinking: Stop negative self-talk to reduce stress." January 21, 2020. https://www.mayoclinic.org/healthy-lifestyle/stress-management/in-depth/positive-thinking/art-20043950

around people who enable you to remain at ground level will only keep you at ground level. Always remember that energy begets energy—it's contagious. Both positive and negative energy can be transferred to whomever they come into contact with.

You were not placed on this earth to be a failure, quitter, or anyone's punching bag. So stop letting life karate kick you around! Pass out a couple roundhouses yourself. Fortify your home by using the principle of feng shui and strengthen your mind with the methods described herein—you'll automatically give yourself a greater chance to live your best life. The whole point of life is to truly enjoy it. The more you love yourself, love from love, not love from hate, the more you can edify others allowing them to see a clearer path to their own self-promotion. We all can win. One must love themselves first to form the right foundation to love anyone else. Only then will you be truly blessed to be a blessing.

Remaining at low altitudes will not enable you to pursue your passion for helping others, whether it's through your nonprofit organization, successful business, or even as a philanthropist in your community. Having the correct attitude, passion, vision, consistency, and stick-to-itiveness are all key ingredients to making your wish come true for helping others. No one said it was going to be easy, nor was it meant to be. You must be up for the challenge with a mindset for winning, or you're going to remain bird feeding those you so passionately care about with crumbs. Or even worse, you'll be the one being hand-fed. And if you're like me, it will drive you up the wall that you aren't doing a lot more for others in need. But in due time, my dear friend, as you become a master imagineer, it will all come together just like the way you painted the positive mental picture in your mind.

"If you can visualize it, if you can dream it, there's some way to do it."
WALT DISNEY

It's all a process that doesn't work when we put the cart before the horse. Life is a cosmic combination, and every move, second, and action places you one step closer or further to either opening windows of opportunity, or pits of agony. It's your positive outlook on life that will guide you in the correct direction. Enjoy every step of the process. You may just write a best-seller about the journey someday.

Surround yourself with people that exude a winning attitude. Seek those with an abundance of positive ambition, zeal, and resiliency so you can tap into their energy and rhythm. You'll know how to spot them by seeing their faith in action as the words they speak comes into existence right before your eyes; their energy is so contagious that their table overflows with blessings that will be tumbling right onto yours. The sweet fruits they continually produce speak for themselves.

Your demeanor is an outward display of your mental approach to life. Having the right attitude is loving everyone and everything good and worthwhile. It's your feelings about yourself, other people, and Mother Nature that weighs in on our quality of life. As mentioned earlier, your confidence is based on how much you believe in yourself or lack thereof. In other words, it's your attitude spiritual report card. When life gives you sour lemons, turn them into sweet, ice-cold lemonade. Stop pouting for long periods when things go bad or when someone says something that you don't like. So, what! Lick your wounds, and keep it pushing. There's going to be tons of lies that will be said about you. Stop allowing petty arguments, especially online, and low-level people to derail you from the BIGGER PICTURE! Yes, it sucks to get used and abused but don't allow scumbags to get the best of you. Enough of that nonsense. No, I don't know what you've been through, but know this—I am much more concerned about where you're heading than where you've been. You must condition your heart and mind, to see the silver lining, or you'll get stuck in the quicksand of depression. It's incredible how starving children still find a way to smile. They still have their power of imagination intact with the hopes of a better tomorrow.

A good attitude is having the right ideas about yourself and the right frame of mind about your position in the world. Many of us think incorrectly, have no written plan, and wonder why things rarely work out. One piece of advice that I'll give (even though this book is flooded with good counsel) is to STOP being so uptight about everything, thinking that everything you don't like has to be expressed—it's a waste of good energy and it destroys good vibes and cripples mean-ingful relationships. Do you have any idea how hard it is to find that special someone who's compatible, loves you, and is trustworthy in the 21st century? It's pretty much near a miracle. Stop and ask yourself if a positive attitude between spouses could affect the divorce rate within our country? I'm sure that if more individuals, and/or couples were consistently positive, the outlook on marriage within the US would be drastically better.

Imagine This:

Imagine catching every pass thrown at you in a football championship game. Imagine making every shot you take from the 3-point line—nothing but net. Swoosh! Imagine each of your business meetings concludes with a lucrative contract and a signing bonus. Imagine every job interview that you've gone af-ter wants to hire you and is willing to pay a higher rate than the industry's average. Imagine each house that you flip remained under the remodeling budget and triples in profit.

As long as you have the correct orientation, you'll still have the up-per hand even when you're having one of those "it can't get any worse" types of days. With that being said, before you decide to go flying off the handle with your mouth, the point must be re-emphasized, remem-ber: Life meets you the way you meet life. Join the fight of life with a new and improved stance rather than running away from it. Instead of throwing in the towel, toss in your hat! Get some skin in the game.

Ask yourself:

"What attitude am I greeting the universe with today?"

What you see in your outer world stems from your inner world. Both worlds are a reflection of each other; they mirror each other mentally, spiritually, and physically. You'll either have a spectacular reflection or a broken mirror. The person who eats right and exercises consistently wants a healthier lifestyle so they can live longer. They'll be able to extend experiencing the natural highs of life through the loving energy of playing with their children, grandchildren, and loved ones. Jogging, working out in a gym, and meditative stretching increases our mental strength in other areas of our lives. And, as we do our weightlifting exercises to develop our biceps, shoulders, six-packs, or quads, there are also meditative exercises we can do throughout the day to strengthen our "mindfulness muscle."

These meditative exercises help us feel our mind in the body more present, more aware, and more focused when we are doing our daily activities. Furthermore, meditative exercises also bring in a much-needed balance into our busy lives, along with greater calmness and crystal-clear clarity. For many of us, we'll finally experience equanimity. The more time we spend sitting with the mind, the more at ease we feel within ourselves. We'll also be able to make the right decisions in perplexing situations.

A person with bad eating habits will eventually have frequent trips to three places: the bathroom, the hospital, and the doctor's office. What they've been consuming over the years will have a gradual impact on their health. At the same time, these two types of individuals will see life differently and will approach their diets with contrasting actions. I bet you thought it was all about sweating and pain to look sexier, a beautiful mind adds to your sexiness.

Meditative Exercises

Working Out: Before the workout, sit down motionless for 1 minute. Take a nice deep breath, in through the nose and out through the mouth. Feel the mind in the body, and then focus on different parts of your body. Notice how the body feels and embrace the feeling whether there's a sense of energy or pain from a previous workout.

Showering: Be aware of how the water feels as it hits your head, your back, your arms. Showering is a good habit to have. Notice which part of the body you wash first, then switch it up. As you step into the shower, be aware of how the water feels as it hits your skin, your hands, your head, your back, and your arms. Is it warm enough? Is it too hot? Too cold? Our mind usually skips town while we take our shower. If your thoughts have wandered, gently pull your attention back to the present and finish washing up.

Eating: Pray before you eat your meal. Give thanks because there are millions of people starving while you sit comfortably at your table or in your car preparing to eat a delicious meal. Pause to bring your attention to the food. Think about where your food has come from, where it was grown, and how it was prepared. Food, whether it's a scrumptious salad with all the bells and whistles or a slab of juicy well-seasoned ribs, usually takes an adventure to get from the farm to your plate. Chew the food slowly, don't wolf down your meal. Take your time to enjoy each spoonful of food, taste, and enjoy the combination of flavors on your palate. Deliciously prepared meals are an art form too!

———

"If you can get nothing better out of the world, get a good dinner out of it, at least."
HERMAN MELVILLE

———

In the fall season, you can look up in the sky and see the beautiful leaves swirl all over the place. You'll eventually see birds flying in perfectly symmetrical, V-shaped formations. They may be swans, geese, cranes, pelicans, or flamingos. The V-shaped formations allow them to conserve energy since each bird flies slightly ahead of the other, creating less wind resistance that enables them to fly further without exerting all of their energy. It's a breathtaking event to watch. You can feel the energy somehow. The beauty of Mother Nature always seems to amaze me. Oftentimes, when these birds are on the move in these large flocks, they migrate nearly 5,000 miles a year to their destination for mating, a better climate, and food. At the end of the day, survival is on their mind. The point here is it's okay to move forward relentlessly with a team, if you must, in order to reach your goals. An African proverb says, "If you want to move fast go alone. If you want to get further go together."

When you're hanging around a circle of eagles, they'll stretch you beyond your comfort zone. They have to move forward and won't let your excuses hold them back. It's in their nature to think big and to see bigger. When you're down and out, eagles are leaders who can see more in you than you see within yourself. The good thing about them is that they won't let you be mediocre. They won't let you settle for a one-room shack when you deserve a mansion. They won't let you be complacent with driving a hooptie that's always breaking down when you should be in an S550 or Bentley. They'll encourage you to dress for success and to throw away the penny loafers. They'll also prevent you from accepting being belittled by your companion. They won't allow you to be comfortable living paycheck to paycheck with your nose barely above water when you should be in a position to leave an inheritance for your children and their children. They'll keep motivating you until you've elevated to their level, or to a position higher than they are. When you reach your goals, they'll also be there to celebrate with you.

Final Thoughts

Self-promotion comes from within first before it can come from any outside sources. Surround yourself with goal-getters if you're truly ready for the next level. Utilize colorology to your advantage in your daily routine to evoke a positive attitude and outlook on life. Find the color that resonates with the personality/energy you'd like to be associated with.

ACTIVATE SELF-PROMOTION IN 5 SIMPLE WAYS

- Start with small promotions with your health. (i.e., go from a plain boring salad to a salad with dried cranberries and almonds with the best tasting dressing money can buy.) Also, consider adding alkaline water to your diet.
- Invest in your spiritual and intellectual growth, and MOVE!
- Promote yourself by titling yourself appropriately: CEO, President, Founder, Mom, Dad, or Child of God.
- Regain your childlike confidence when nothing was impossible.
- Avoid dream killers (DK's) by any means necessary. They're usually family members and friends.

Bonus Tip:

- Silver Spoon. Purchase a nice set of thick and shiny silverware to eat with. Retire the old scratched up and bent ones. You'll love the difference in how they'll make you feel. Besides, you'll impress your guests. Cost: $15-$20. Benefits: priceless.

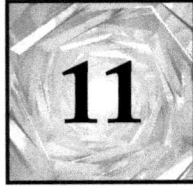

11

WALK INTO YOUR VICTORY

*T*HE WAY YOU WALK INTO YOUR DAY IS USUALLY HOW it will end. When I wake up in the mornings, nine out of ten times, the first thing I say is, "Thank you God, for another awesome day that you have given me. This is the day that I AM going to be victorious!" The day hasn't even begun yet, so what am I doing? Very simple. Preparing myself to have a great day. I begin most of my days with drinking a cup of water and praying while facing the sun or a window, then I go into meditation, or vice versa, if possible. This is done to acknowledge the everyday miracles of life, the sun rising, and to internalize the magnificent power of it.

As a matter of fact, I truly believe the original purpose of why our ancestors of Kemet gave so much reverence to the sun and its warmth was for a deep purpose. The sun represented Our Creator giving the world a warm hug. They overstood that the sun was the single most powerful entity impacting the planet. It is also my belief, that after years of studying the hieroglyphics, artwork, and temples, they woke up early every day to absorb the calmness of the sun's morning glory;

this relaxing state set the tone for the day and prepared the mind, body, and spirit for what they needed to accomplish that day or for the near future.

It doesn't matter if I am home or traveling abroad, praying and meditation are both vitally important to my existential soul. It's the daily food that my spirit requires to extend my happiness. We have to feed our spirit the right things because it's not going to feed itself. We are living in a world suffering from both a spiritual and moral famine. Let's not forget to mention, common sense isn't common anymore. We're conditioned to feed our bodies but not our souls. As our souls starve for nourishment, our Inner-G is growing weak. Praying, singing melodies, and meditating on peace and prosperity are ways to bless our inner being free of charge. The only cost is investing your time in the aforementioned activities, and many of us cannot afford to ignore them any longer.

Additionally, let go of your phone! Most people, especially our youth, wake up and jump straight on their phone as if it's glued to their palms. As a matter of fact, they sleep with their phones and tablets in their hands. It's a crying shame that many parents are unknowingly allowing these devices to raise their children meanwhile it's robbing them of their common sense. Many adults are guilty of this as well. These mobile devices have become gods and idols to most people by the way; they were designed to keep our eyes glued on the screens for as long as possible; as we're having 'fun' the powers that be are using these digital idols to persuade our behavior, thinking, and shopping habits. We worship them to such a degree that we'll often sacrifice our last dollars to obtain one. We can't think without them. We panic when we leave our home without our phones. We feel whole only when we have our smartphones fully charged and in our hands. This is ridiculous! It's a dangerous habit that causes us to miss out on so many of life's most precious moments. The situation has gotten so bad that robbers, thieves, and other degenerates seek out people distracted with their phones that they wait for the opportune time to attack.

This phenomenon isn't only happening in the big cities of New York or London, but try getting on a subway and notice the number of people who are tuned in to their phones—nearly everyone. The Incredible Hulk could sit right next to us, and we wouldn't even notice. The simple fact is that these phones have all of our banking, medical, and business information, all of which explains how anyone could be so attached to their device. Too much of anything isn't good for you. I'd say it's better to spend less time binge-watching TV shows, texting, and scrolling on social media and more time meditating, intentional reading, and praying for the good we wish to be, to have, and to maintain. The moment your self-worth or happiness is based on material things and money, you're in big trouble. It's time to re-evaluate your values by getting in tuned with our spiritual consciousness and experience more of all-consciousness, peace, unity, love and freedom from the ugliness that fear brings. There are plenty of wealthy people that are extremely unhappy because they've allowed their finances to imprison them from the simple joys of life. We must debunk the theory that money makes you a happier and better person, or the lack thereof makes you any less of a human being. The quality of a person is based on their value system. Our values determine our behavior, our actions, and with the wrong values comes a life of chaos and despair.

Instead of sending that text or making that last call before you sleep, close your eyes and think about which components of your day you enjoyed the most? Who do you want to be a blessing to? Why and how? You must end your day with the same positive vibrations you started it with. On the other hand, let's say your day started on the wrong side of the bed, you have the opportunity to redirect that energy before the beautiful sunrises again with you on the right side this time. If yesterday was unpleasant, it's not the end of the world. Take a deep breath and remind yourself that tomorrow is a new day and with it comes a second chance to maintain, and build up your new positive thoughts throughout the day. In your world, you are the director. The buck starts and stops with you!

ENERGY VAMPIRE SLAYER

Avoid negative people! Run, duck, and hide from them. Receiving early morning calls, reading/replying to text messages, and emails from toxic people is a no-no. You may want to cease communicating with them completely, if possible. Look at it this way: negative people are raging bulls that are trying to knock you off your A-game. Their goal is to completely wipe you out of existence. You are your own responsibility, and it's imperative to take charge of who and what is around your energy. There are people that give us negative charges and then others who uplift us with a positive voltage. Having this type of consciousness will bless your socks off and literally save your dreams by selecting the latter.

The enemy will send countless arrows your way. Each attack is a direct threat to your peace of mind, physical body, and emotions. All of which are pains that are represented by little cracks upon your spiritual and mental vase. A vase can always be glued back into one piece, but the scars will remain, whether they are visible or not. One of your top priorities in this life is to reduce the number of self-inflicted wounds cast upon your vase. We are all pottery made with unique pieces of history, light, sun, stars, and lots of love glued together with magic, powerful music, and inspiring words.

Whenever there is a purpose, expect opposition. There are no exceptions to this rule. The greater the purpose, the greater the opposition. People will come at you sideways like the bishop on the chessboard. Treat them like raging bulls. Guess who's going to be the bullfighter? You are! You're the matador. Let them come at you with all of their negativity while you gracefully stand, baiting them to keep charging toward your red flag. The actual name for a matador in Spanish is *matador de Toros* (killer of bulls). They may think they have you cornered, however, you'll just let them run right out of your way. Hopefully, they'll find themselves out of your life.

There are people that are so unhappy with their lives that they look for others to dump their trash on. Are you a garbage basket or landfill? I don't think so. WE ARE GREATNESS! Never make time for people's negativity. You have to audit your circle and figure out who the energy vampires are in your life. If you're not careful, before you know it, they'll slowly suck every ounce of ambition, energy, and joy out of you. There's a big difference between people that make time to talk to you, and the people that talk to you only on their free time—know the difference. I just happen to be a professional energy vampire slayer. If you practice the following steps, you'll become one too!

3 SIMPLE WAYS TO IDENTIFY ENERGY VAMPIRES: (DRAMA QUEENS & KINGS)

➲ They're always taking from others and proud of never giving something in return.
➲ They're emotional rollercoasters, constantly requiring your immediate attention, resources, and time.
➲ You usually feel drained after speaking with them whether in person, through text, or over the phone.

All of the aforementioned are extremely unhealthy for your world and bright future. Make it your business to remove these energy thieves from your Winning Equation.

For example, one of the first nice apartments that I rented was a beautiful two-bedroom, two-bathroom condominium in Lauderhill (West Fort Lauderdale, Florida) for a reasonable price of $900 a month the first year. Everyone else were paying around $1,300 for the rent. The landlord, an old Jewish woman, was at first, as kind as can be. After a couple of years as her tenant, she had become too comfortable with calling me during the early morning hours for various reasons, especially if my check didn't get to her by the third of the month. I took her calls out of respect for my elders, but it got to a point where I realized I needed to put my foot down to protect my peace of mind since she was clearly taking advantage of my politeness. Once it dawned on me that she was manipulating my day I stopped taking her calls. It felt great deciding to ignore her early bird tactics, and I never felt bad about it. The mornings are designed to build up your energy, not to destroy it. Once I mustered up the strength to screen her calls, it hit me that I should've done that a long time ago but it's better late than never.

After that small victory, I got the revelation that there was a long list of people I needed to start ignoring altogether. The sunrise hours of the day are designed to strengthen our spirit to deal with the characters that cross our path during work and within our daily routines. Sometimes the average days turn out to be anything but normal. We all know what type of energy and spirit our co-workers operate in; some of them seem to be working under demonic possession and probably are.

You may need to start creating a list of negative people to ignore in the mornings. It might be necessary to completely ostracize them from your life. Your spirituality is the most important part of your growth and development. As surprising as it may sound, I am far from perfect; however, I spend a tremendous amount of time investing in my spirituality through prayer, meditation, soaking up wisdom from my elders, feeding the temporarily homeless, and reading edifying books. Watching football or other sporting events for hours at a time doesn't appeal to me when I could be working on making my millions seeing that those athletes are already rich. Watching sports and the seventy thousand fans rooting them on will not get me or you where we want to be. The average person watches a staggering 78,000 hours of TV in their lifetime, and 2,943 hours of their life deciding what to watch; and this is not including YouTube videos. So much time and energy are spent on watching a screen when we could be working on our goals instead. Therefore, I reduced my viewing time, and often eliminated watching the games altogether; over the years I've developed a strange habit of "watching" the games while the television is on mute as I worked on my projects. Even though I am a former football player turned football junky, I refrain from allowing my love for the sport to override my love for accomplishing my dreams.

There're so many variables in life that are geared toward breaking us down. As for me, I was convinced that I had to contend for my life. If I were to survive and, more importantly, thrive in this life, I knew the best weapons I possessed were the words I spoke, my praises to the Almighty God, and a positive attitude. You can't tell me that I'm not balling, blessed, and highly favored! Some folks will actually get offended if you tell them they're rich, or "balling". Why get upset? Wouldn't you one day want to be financially rich or at least stable enough that you don't have to check your bank account balance every time you need to go grocery shopping? Or when you're at the gas pump? Why not speak good health and wealth into existence even if you'll living in an abandoned building? This message is specifically for you. Sometimes we have to fake it until we make it since that's what many of us are doing anyway. However, if we're honest with ourselves, many of our actions are detrimental to our future, and for that reason, it's impossible to thrive when disinvesting in ourselves. For the life of me, I couldn't understand why speaking financial prosperity into people's lives offended them. You're a perfect candidate for a Mental Makeover if you get offended by someone speaking positively towards you.

Every single day, I deliberately speak blessings into the universe with words of affirmation with my favorite phrase, "Today Is A Great Day to Be Alive!" To be honest, I don't feel like every day is going to be a great one, but the truth is if you were to miss a morning, you'd no longer be among the living. There were many days and nights I felt like crap. Feelings vary and change for some regularly. It's dangerous to allow the days of your life to be based on solely feelings. That's when having the right mindset kicks in. It's your backup battery when you need a jolt of positive vibes. Sometimes you must clap yourself out of depression. Clap long and hard for as long as you have to until you wake up that sleeping giant within. The right people in your corner are extra sources from your positive energy bank to back you up when you feel your Inner-G is starting to diminish, which is normal. Don't worry, it's still there. Sometimes we just get tired and need a small boost to turn things around. True friends are there to be a blessing to you by speaking words of encouragement when you're down and out. They know when you need an anointed hug or a helping hand to pull you up from the ground. Nothing makes a friend happier than to see their friend(s) walk into their vision and achieve their goals.

Equally important, the friends that have made it into the latter part of your adult life are the battle-tested. Thank God for good friends because a lot of times they are there for you when your family isn't. Most of the friends I grew up with aren't in communication with me today. Their outlook on life never improved, and it took too much of my energy to explain to myself why I should maintain our relationships knowing that we're on completely different wavelengths. One of the most common responses many of them would give when asked, "How's it going?" or something hipper like, "What's happening?" and the reply would be, "Same stuff, different day", "I can't catch a break for nothing in the world", "Another day, another dollar", "I'm broke as a joke", or "If it wasn't for bad luck, I wouldn't have any luck at all". You get the picture. It doesn't seem like a pretty painting being painted, does it?

Another circle of friends would say, "God is good, and His mercy will endure forever!" "I'm blessed and highly favored!" "Today is going to be another great day!" "A miracle happens every day!" or "Today might be my day!" Whenever they called me in the morning, I got excited to answer the phone or to give them a ring because we knew that we could expect positive energy from each other. The difference between the energy around the words from my circle of friends was night and day. Words can literally create an avalanche of darkness or an overflow of blessings into our everyday lives. Even if your life may have seemed to be destroyed by an evil act, or an unfortunate turn of events, you can still pull yourself up by your own will and see the silver lining. As long as you can maintain your positivity, you'll be empowering yourself to see better days—they're right ahead. Just remain positive long enough and you will see them on the horizon coming your way!

The same people who usually started their conversations with "Another day, another dollar" are still working mediocre jobs or are on the streets robbing and selling drugs, which is selling a piece of their soul with every deal. I know since I've walked miles in that ugly pair of shoes. However, I threw them away as far as these 260lb bench pressing arms could muster. Daddy got on a new pair of shoes! One would think that after years of heartaches and run-ins with the law that my old friends would eventually change the way they made ends meet. Nope. They are still speaking those same words of defeat through every outlet they have whether it's in face-to-face conversations, text messages, phone calls, social media, and even their comments on YouTube videos.

On the other hand, most of my friends and associates start their conversations with positive energy. They'll say things like "A Miracle Is Going to Happen Today!" "I Am Blessed and Highly Favored!" or "God is soooooo good!" All of them are rich in spirit, successful entrepreneurs, or are working at high-level positions, making a hefty six to seven-figure salary. I guarantee you these folks know what's happening. The only time we are lost in our world is when we are not in control of it. It's not a good life when the bill collectors, employers, and other external factors dictate our happiness and activities within our daily lives.

After all these years, I can't help but believe our words can either make or break us because I've seen it happen unfailingly time after time. We've been lied to. Sticks and stones can break our bones, but words can absolutely crush us. However, words by the right person can guide you in the correct direction. Those with confidence talk differently. Winners speak like winners in view of the fact that we prepare ourselves to be successful in whatever we do. Losers speak like losers as if they expect to fail but deep down inside, we all want to win. Losing isn't what winners dwell upon. Michael Jordan, six-time NBA Champion, and MVP in each year of those NBA Finals knows a lot about winning championships. He talked about his mental strategy for taking game-winning shots in his documentary *The Last Dance*. He stated, "Why would I be nervous before taking a shot that I haven't taken yet?"

Michael has a great point and as mentioned, winners speak with a certain swag that can't be bought. Confidence is paid for with sweat equity through the battlefields of life, giving us the necessary assertiveness to take on bigger challenges.

Final Thoughts

Instead of saying, "I can't," say, "I can!" The Little Engine That Could kept saying to herself, "I think I can. I think I can," as she continued moving forward. She went from thinking she couldn't tread the high mountain to believing in herself as she MOVED forward. She challenged herself and was victorious. "I thought I could, I think I can, I know I can!" We were taught this story as children so we could begin believing in our abilities and not give up before putting in our best effort. Walk into your victory—TAKE THE SHOT!

5 WAYS TO MENTALLY WALK INTO YOUR VICTORY

⮞ Start everyday with positive words to yourself.
⮞ Become an energy vampire slayer. Get more people with a positive charge into your life.
⮞ Clap to yourself when you're down. Awaken the the giant within.
⮞ Believe that you can with all of your willpower and you will achieve it.
⮞ Speak with boldness. Walk confidently. Embrace your victories.

I'M READY TO WIN BIG

Hold up your mirror in one hand and apply your makeup
and hair grease with the other. While doing this, stop
for a second to think about what role you will try to play
in life? Clown or villain? Failure or champion?

Rule Number 1 - Never Be Number Two!

KNOWING WHAT MOTIVATES YOU ALLOWS YOU TO position yourself with a mindset to be productive. Acting on those motivators enables your heart to develop the fortitude to take on any and all challenges. You just have to keep pushing past the hard times until you've pushed those mountains out of the way. Remembering to bless those who helped you win along the way is an act of high honor. This small act of gratitude shows you have a heart of gold and not of stone. If you're not careful though, you'll boast and brag about yourself without thinking of those who sacrificed to help you along the way. Acting as if you made everything happen by yourself is an illusion that stems from selfishness. The same people you stepped on going up the ladder of success will be the same people you meet on your way back down.

With this in mind, instead of doing a lot of talking, allow your actions to speak for themselves. Actions speak much louder than words ever will. Acts of honor speak volumes about your character. For instance, I often find myself reflecting on how my Great Aunt Jacqueline used to have dinner waiting for me once I got home from school during my junior year in college. At the time, I was a financially challenged college student, and for a semester, I lived in Little Haiti, one of the roughest urban districts in Miami. She was in her mid-eighties, nearly blind, and would gently knock on the door with her frail hands and softly call out my name in the evenings to see if I made it back from school. Four days a week I had to get up at 5:00 am in order to catch the long train ride across three counties to reach Boca Raton at 6:00 am.

Her love reminded me that I was still somebody important, when I was at my lowest, and I could not wait to return the favor when I got back on my feet. Imagine being treated as a king when you felt like a peasant. She had no idea how much she motivated me through her acts of love and kindness. My heart dropped when I witnessed her put an X where her signature should have been written on the medical document that I translated for her in Creole. She had no formal education and wasn't taught how to write so she signed her name with an X. With her poor vision, I took the liberty of showing her how to write the letter J instead. She enjoyed the lesson, and it was my honor to do so.

Honoring those who mentored or supported you reminds them that their good deed wasn't a waste of time. Chances are, one day, you'll be in a good position to be a blessing to someone else. Seek out the teachers, old friends, mentors, and mother and father figures who supported you and your family during those tough times. Visit them, take them to dinner, surprise them with a pair of movie tickets, pay their car note, mortgage, or bless them with a gift card. Do anything to show them that you treasure their support. It will be a blessing to both of you when you're finally able to pay it forward. They may just need you to lift them up this time around. I honored my Great Aunt Jacqueline because she honored me. By doing so, it gave my rough journey a boost of spiritual energy that helped me push through an extremely dark time of my young adult life. In other words, when we honor others it gives us power.

To be a winner, you must develop the heart of a champion! How bad do you want to win? Please, please, please don't say "by any means necessary" since that means you'll be willing to sell your soul and only God knows how far you'll go. How does one sell their soul? By stealing, killing, and selling their body, not to mention destroying others to get what and where you want to go. These vile acts don't have one shred of righteousness within them. Now, if your response was "<u>by any righteous</u> means necessary," means that you're willing to burn the midnight oil on your computer typing and researching, getting out of bed early to pick up where you left off the previous night, reading the necessary books, making the calls to get new clients, and acting upon the investments you were advised to partake in.

Champions don't give up or give in. We find a way to hang in the fight and hold onto our resolve, whether it be a sporting event, a corporate setting, or an actual battlefield with guns, tanks, horses, and flying aliens shooting laser beams. We make it happen! The new normal that we've been forced into presents an unprecedented terrain. It's times like these that we should take advantage of to redefine ourselves and lift those who are throwing in the towel, both young and old. Faith is a currency that pays large dividends to those who have it to invest and spend!

"Don't punch your opponent, punch through your opponent!"
CUS D'AMATO

Cus D'Amato, arguably the greatest trainer of all-time, taught Mike Tyson, the youngest heavyweight boxing champion in history. Mr. Tyson had to repeat four intentional sentences (S.B.E.) throughout his training from the age of 13 in order to promote himself from guaranteed obscurity and to achieve the impossible. Cus also forced him to read the biography of Alexander The Great, king of the ancient Greek kingdom of Macedonia in Europe; he wanted him to read his story for inspiration since the ancient warrior king had a winning mindset and an ambition larger than life to rule the world. Cus wasn't just a coach, mentor, and foster parent, he was also an expert in psychology and embedded into each of his boxer's head that they're going to be champions. This resonated extremely well with the young boxer because all of his life he was labeled a loser, a criminal, and told that he'd be dead or in prison like the rest of his friends. He was determined to turn the table. All he needed was genuine love, attention, and proper guidance like most young children from urban communities growing up in broken homes, as we speak.

Therefore, he trained like a champion almost to the point that he was obsessed with becoming the best that ever stepped into the ring. By the time he was 20, Tyson was wearing his first of three championship belts. He became the first heavyweight boxer to simultaneously hold the WBA, WBC and IBF titles, as well as the only heavyweight to unify them in succession. Iron Mike successfully defended his world heavyweight title an amazing ten times, including highly anticipated bouts with former champions Larry Holmes and Michael Spinks. Before Don King and Robin Givens sunk their teeth deep into the champ's mind and bank account, Cus was able to instill an incredible lesson on the mind power of self-belief into the young boxer. Cus was able to turn a teenage punk known for his street fighting and temper into a disciplined bona fide gladiator with character and skill that struck fear into all of his opponents. Mike won an estimated $400 million over the course of his illustrious career.

You're ready to win, now, I bet! Here are Cus's magical four sentences:

1. I'm champion because I am determined to be champion.
2. I believe in what I'm doing.

3. I cannot be dissuaded.
4. I will not be dissuaded.

Ready to win big, yet? I hope so since you know by now that you have the right attitude, put your faith out there, and refuse to be denied. You have to take jurisdiction of your mind, and your time—it's yours! The mind is too powerful for you to allow it to dominate you with a laissez-faire demeanor. Give your mind no way out! If you are prone to quit and complain when things get hard—*burn all the ships* so you will have no choice but to keep moving forward until you find the treasure on your life's M.A.P. Once you've reached your toughest goals, you'll experience an immeasurable sense of accomplishment by virtue of you refusing not to throw in the towel. The tranquility of triumph is a rewarding feeling that gets better and better. You have to see yourself at the top and not at the bottom. In your mind and spirit, envision the victory of achieving your goals even when your bank account is on E and only lint in your pocket. You have to *lambano* your dreams! Like Apostles Edward, and Yvette Brinson would always say in their sermons with big smiles on their faces, "You have to *LAMBANO* that thing!"

Lambano is a Greek word meaning to take what is one's own, to take to oneself, or to make one's own. You have to take hold of your vision with the fierceness of a Peregrine Falcon diving at the mind-blowing rate of speed of 200 mph from the highest peak to grab an unsuspecting salmon in the lake. Keep going, stay focused, and you shall win! This is the true secret to success! Your dreams are the juicy salmons in the lake.

You see, both the falcon and eagle know that they have to catch fish, squirrels, and small mammals if they're going to survive. They're even more aggressive when it comes to hunting for their chicks since they know their babies are in the nest hungry and expecting a good meal. Parents know this feeling all too well. You must become more aggressive when it comes to the things you want to accomplish before you can be any good to your family. You can't be passive about it. YOU HAVE TO *LAMBANO* THAT THING!

Optimists ride the waves that they create, big or small. Pessimists get knocked down over and over. See yourself grabbing your dreams with both hands and biting them with your teeth. Pull them from the spiritual realm into the physical realm, from inside your mind to manifestation. Add the necessary feelings and fierceness as if you're pulling in a 915 lb. marlin from your 520-foot private yacht. Repetition of the aforementioned is extremely important to make your Winning Equation work in pursuit of reaching your M.A.P.'s destination. I know you just read it but read it again with your spiritual eyes. This time, practice the mindfulness exercise by seeing yourself as a falcon grabbing your dreams from the spiritual world, speaking them into existence, and slowly pulling them out of the lake into reality with all of your willpower.

10 Traits of a Champion Mindset

We Don't...

1. Talk much about what we lack. We do what must be done with what we have.
2. Make excuses. We make it happen.
3. Complain. You can count on us in the trenches.
4. Focus on the past. We are consistently focused on the future.
5. Fold when trouble comes. We toss in our hat, not our towels.
6. Dwell on our problems. We ponder on ways to solve them.

We...

7. Look at adversity as a sign that we're heading in the right direction.

8. Have an incredible ability to focus on the bottom line to win.
9. Prepare ourselves to have the best possible outcome.
10. Don't quit until the mission is complete.

A perfect example of someone who refused to be denied and dared to face all their challenges head-on is the Bahamian track star Shaunae Miller-Uibo. Even at the young age of twenty-two, the professional sprinter ran the race of her life at the 2016 Olympics in Rio, Brazil. I've seen plenty of great races but never witnessed as much grit on a track field prior compared to what she displayed. Ms. Miller refused to accept second place in anything she placed her time and energy into—she convinced herself that she was going to win. She was determined to not take no for an answer! She decreed and declared that she was going to go out as a champion and she put her faith where her dream was. Ms. Miller was up against the women's 200 and 400-meter juggernaut Allyson Michelle Felix, a nine-time Olympic medalist, who was by far the favorite in the race. Knowing she was the underdog may have played to Shaunae's advantage, relieving her of the pressure the other popular runners who were facing with their multimillion-dollar endorsements and sponsorships.

Ms. Felix was on track to be the first track and field athlete to win another gold medal with her sixth after that race.[51] But not so fast. The two went toe-to-toe all the way down to the final stretch as if it were the twelfth round of a heavyweight boxing match. As Ms. Felix was about to cross the finish line, Ms. Miller surprisingly dove forward like a falcon. The officials had to conduct a rare photo finish judgment to determine which track queen won the race. Lo and behold, Shaunae Miller pulled off a stunning upset for the gold medal in grand fashion

---

[51] DiGiacomo, Paul. "Allyson Felix: American Athlete" https://www.britannica.com/biography/Allyson-Felix

with a split time of 49.44! Ms. Felix was just a millisecond (.07 seconds) behind her with a 49.51 finish.

It was an incredibly close race and possibly the best race ever displayed at the Olympic Games. In 2016, Shaunae ended up finally becoming an Olympic champion. Even if she doesn't win another contest, that was a run for the angels! She gave it all she had and left everything on the track. This is the type of winning attitude one must have toward life in this competitive world if you're going to win big. It doesn't matter if you're aiming to get your business to the next level or on a quest to find the one you're going to marry. Put in one hundred percent effort in your preparation so that when the time is right—you'll be ready to seize the golden opportunity.

Most of us, especially her critics, don't know Ms. Miller's backstory behind the dive. A point often overlooked, back in the 2012 Olympics, she lost the 400meter race due to an injury. She had four years to replay the agony of defeat over and over, possibly a million times in her mind. The pain of losing could be either torment or motivation to practice even harder. She didn't need a Skinner's Box to know that this time around she was going to experience the thrill of victory in view of the fact that almost winning doesn't feel good at all. During the 2016 Olympics, she wanted a different ending to her story, and she gave it all she had, literally. Even if she had lost, the effort was an unmistakable heart of a champion. As goal-getters, that's the type of attitude we'd want on our team, someone who will give you all they have to win fair and square with nothing left behind!

"Care about what other people think and you will always be their prisoner."
LAO TZU

Ms. Miller received both praise and criticism for diving for the gold. Did she care? Heavens no! I stand with her seeing that if she had cared about the world's opinion (the press, haters, detractors, or etc.) of her then she wouldn't have made that drastic, last-second move. She knew deep down in her gut she was not going to leave the 2016 Olympics without that victory. That was the mission. That's how bad you have to want it. Eric Thomas, the motivational speaker, once said "When you want to succeed as bad as you want to breathe, then you'll be successful." Had Allyson dove at the finish line, she would've won the race, however, history will forever remember the champion, not the runner-up.

It's important to realize that it's too easy to get caught up in what others think when they don't give a rat's poop about us. Some folks wouldn't care if they saw you eating out of the trash can because they'll take a picture and post it on their social media pages for laughs and likes. It's a low-down crying shame that I actually witnessed this first-hand. Some people will probably donate a hot meal and offer you a clean bed to rest your head, but it will take the drastic situation of homelessness to get help. This ought not to be the case. Let's make it a mission to offer a hand to those that we can help before they hit rock bottom and thrown into the streets.

I once saw a high school friend, Travis, at a homeless shelter I was volunteering at for Thanksgiving. It felt like I was punched in the gut to see him in that condition when I gave him a juice and a water bottle in the food line. With high energy, I told him to keep his head up and that better days were ahead. I also gave him my business card in hopes he would call me so that I could see how, together, we could help get his life back on track. Travis was a very outgoing, funny, handsome, and well-dressed young man while in high school, up until the day we graduated in 1999. He was probably one of the most popular students. Unfortunately, he wasn't the only outgoing, young black man I knew from school or the neighborhood that ended up living on the streets, addicted to drugs, dead, or in prison. Over the years, I've bumped into over a dozen of them that fell into hard times. Success isn't guaranteed to anyone, but failure is when we fail to do our best with our God-given talents. We all have something that distinguishes us from everyone else. Pinpoint what that talent is, master it, market it, and profit from it. Do it for the pride, and not for the money. When you're the best at what you do, you provide something people need in excellence, the money will come in abundance. There is no better marketing than word-of-mouth and that comes with superb customer service.

Quitters and the poor will always be among us, but that doesn't mean you have to be one of them. How are we going to be a blessing to the poverty-stricken if we are broken down and disgusted? People give up all the time; they check out on life and settle for the streets if they don't take their own life first. Suicides are committed because no one was there to talk them out of it at a critical moment of their life. They used the power of free will to make the most fatal of choices one can make. Who knows, maybe Bryce Gowdy just needed a little love at a time when life was confusing to him before he saw the train approaching. Perhaps 9-year-old McKenzie Adams wanted the reassurance from her mom that she was a beautiful princess, and not the vile names her classmates labeled her with before she took her last breath.

There are many ways to deal with life's hardships, and devoting quality time to your dreams and goals is the best reaction to have. For others, having the wrong attitude and escaping the pain with destructive behaviors become their only real motivation in life. You can complain and feel sorry for yourself but that doesn't help one iota. Complaining only perpetuates the problem by initiating the Law of Attraction in the wrong way. Turning to a life of drugs and abuse is a logical option for those that convinced themselves that they're trapped in an inescapable dark space. There is a way out, but it will take people like you and I carrying the torch of love to share our light. We must give those that are lost in the dark a spark so that they can find their own way.

Growing up in a society that once believed that it takes a village to raise a child, I know that I'm blessed. If it weren't for the collective efforts of my mentors over the years, like my mom, Queen Rosette Pierre (We Miss You), Brother Willie Cameron, College Guidance Counselor, Mrs. Pamela Byrd-Livingston, my middle and high school track coaches, Coach Robert Hall (Rest In Power), Coach Corey Wilson, my fifth-grade teacher Ms. Sonja Wyche, and the many stellar afterschool programs I attended, I probably would've checked out a long time ago.

Now, with everything going on in the world today that is so fast and confusing, we must find a way to incorporate the village culture again to help guide our youth in the right direction. It's up to the village to love, to discipline, and to reward every child; without the extra attention and love that they require we'll continue seeing them crash into dead ends. Brother Willie and his wife invested their time, love, wisdom, and old-fashioned finger-licking home cooking into me. Yearning to be a success in my faith, I decided to select Brother Willie as my spiritual mentor. There was a desire in me to properly balance my career and spiritual life; it was through his network I was able to work directly with Brandon Marshall, former NFL star, to provide a few kids his autographed footballs and Chicago Bears jersey.

Money and success don't mix well with people that aren't well grounded. Anyone can be financially rich, and be piss poor morally at the same time. An abundance of money can easily turn from a blessing to a curse in the wrong hands. We see it all the time with professional athletes, entertainers, and politicians who seemingly had it all but, in the end, lost everything. That is why this work is subtitled "Activating Your Mind, Body, and Spirit". I wanted people to not only be healthy upstairs but to be solid all around.

Besides, even lottery winners have been known to be worse off financially than they were before winning their state's lotto. Believe it or not, lottery winners without a financial advisor are more likely to declare bankruptcy within three-to-five years than the average American.[52] Do yourself

---

[52] Hart, Ryan, "What Percentage of Lottery Winners Go Broke? (Plus 35 More Statistics)" December 3, 2018. https://www.ryanhart.org/lottery-winner-statistics/

a favor and find a mentor. You may not ever think that you'll make another awful decision, but take it from me, it happens to the best of us. And if you do, finding someone with experience in your situation or where you desire to be will prove instrumental in helping you advance. For instance, let's say you want to be a thriving entrepreneur, find a business mentor. Want to be happily married, find a happy husband or a wife to seek wisdom from. How about a successful becoming a real-estate agent, find a real-estate guru to guide you through the ups and downs of the commercial and residential markets. All you have to do is reach out to a couple of people that specialize in your areas of interest. Your energies will connect in the give and take relationship for knowledge. Indeed, ask and you shall receive.

"When the student is ready, the teacher will appear."
BUDDHA SIDDHARTHA GUATAMA SHAKYAMUNI

In conclusion, life doesn't owe you a thing. You have to go out and make it happen. Be ambitious. Be openminded. Don't quit. You've been given the green print from the lives of several larger than life individuals on what it takes to win in this world. The past is the past, and it's my prayer that you're presently more concerned with the future. Plan, plan, plan, and when you're done—plan some more. The more detailed you are with your goals, the better your chances are for success since your vision will be crystal clear. Remember, you can increase your chances of success by over 1000% by writing your goals down. Challenge yourself by giving your dreams a life line date to be accomplished. Speak your goals frequently until it comes to its fruition. It's okay to have only one goal written down, but make it a dream so big that it would be impossible to accomplish on your own.

The impossible is made possible by the one who truly believes that it is possible. Treasure your divinity so that your Inner-G can get to work. You've been empowered to be a god over anything that is causing you problems. You're a god over your health, your fears, your troubles, and your finances. Don't give away your God-power by stressing and cursing your blessings away. Even if you're living in a shelter or haven't been able to pay your mortgage or rent at this very moment, think and operate from a position of abundance knowing that you are a child of the Most High God. The Creator of everything and all things from the heavens to here on earth is on your side. You possess an incredible amount of spiritual strength to take on the world, if only you'd put your faith in action.

Take the time to grab a pen or pencil and concentrate on writing out the future you deserve to have and desire to become. Pray over it. Meditate on the good you want to see, and what action is needed on your part so that the universe will correspond, accordingly. Get excited to be, to do, and to have the good you desire, then go out and get it! Everything comes with time. The best meals sometimes take a little longer to cook, since the seasoning needs to fully marinate but they're well worth the wait.

Ecclesiastes 3:1–5 reminds us that there's a time for everything
and a season for every activity under the heavens:
a time to be born and a time to die,
a time to plant and a time to uproot,
a time to kill and a time to heal,
a time to tear down and a time to build,
a time to weep and a time to laugh,
a time to mourn and a time to dance,
a time to scatter stones and a time to gather them.

And if I may add to the following to this equation…
There's also time to win,
a time to be victorious,
a time to get rich,

a time to volunteer,

a time to love,

a time to be loved,

a time for no retreat and no surrender,

and a time to see a winner in the mirror.

The ancient principles of Ma'at (aka MAAT), which predate the Bible, reminds us to keep our hearts as light as a feather so that we can live in peace and prosperity in this life and in the next. Walking into your purpose could be exactly what your family must have to get over the generational poverty hump. It is time to gather those stones from the lake of abundance and toss in your hat, again, I say. Each stone symbolizes those ideas you gave up on a long time ago, those ideas that people told you were stupid and wouldn't work are coming back to you. The ripples in the water represents the smile of your benevolent ancestors and the universe rooting you on. With enough energy force from your efforts, the short-lived ripples can turn into long lasting waves. Match the frequency of the reality you want to obtain, and you cannot help but get that reality. Most people won't understand your vision since your dreams were too massive for them to grasp. Never minimize your dreams to fit another person's small reality. Your greatness is a threat to the common mind.

5 STEPS TO CREATE YOUR OWN WAVES

- ⮑ Determine what motivates you and intentionally use it as fuel.
- ⮑ Take ownership of your dreams. Then lambano them!
- ⮑ Be consistent. Start working on your ideas with one action and watch it build.
- ⮑ Find a mentor in your field of interest that you can connect well with.
- ⮑ Reach out to someone in dire need of help. Blessing them will bless you.
- ⮑ Take small steps, the flow will increase into big waves. Have fun riding them!

Your triumphs are the antidote to the pain and depression caused by your past that's living rent-free on your psyche. Dust off those stinking thinking ideas from your mind to set your Mental Makeover in motion. Allow this work to be part of the answer to your timidness. Be bold and stretch your tent as far as you can see. Throw your net further than you've ever done before. We never know what blessings The Creator has in store for us. Dare to fly higher and higher. Utilize your Inner-G power and you shall activate the warrior within that is begging to breathe. All you have to do is smile with confidence, keep pushing forward, and never give up. Slow down if you must, but never ever give up. You are born to be courageous!

In conclusion, for real this time, (laughing out loud), in the words of Dr. Martin Luther King, Jr., "If you can't fly, run. If you can't run, walk. If you can't walk, crawl. But by all means — KEEP MOVING!"

Welcome to Your Beginning! Many Blessings...

ABOUT THE AUTHOR

KING KEVIN DORIVAL IS AN AFRICAN-HAITIAN BORN and raised in sunny Fort Lauderdale, Florida and now resides in Atlanta, Georgia, a dream come true! He is a trailblazer that wears many hats, as an entrepreneur, filmmaker, youth chess mentor, international speaker, author of three nonfiction books, and spent most of his professional career as an Internet Marketing Manager for small to large Fortune 500 corporations. Mr. Dorival walked away from corporate America to own and operate a full-service cleaning business in 2020 in the midst of the epidemic. In 2013, he founded *Courage To Believe International (C2B), Inc.*, a 501(c)3, nonprofit organization that teaches the youth how to create strategies in life with the game of chess through their *C2B Chess Club & Youth Mentoring Program and* Annual Black on Black Crime Solutions Panel; the organization's mission is to circumvent the school-to-prison pipeline and the suicide rate amongst the youth in the urban communities.

Mr. Dorival has written three books: *Courage to Believe: Never Give Up, Keep Moving Forward, 7 Types of Queens, Kings Desire*, and *The Winner In The Mirror*. He is a graduate of Florida Atlantic University, where he received his bachelor's degree in Political Science and minor in Marketing. In his downtime, he enjoys family time, watching movies, volunteering, working out, and reading stories of ancient and modern-day African leaders. His next two books will be something special for children, *Prince Peter & The Sparkling Magic Book.* The other book will be entitled, *7 Types of Kings, Queen's Desire.*

Connect via Online Networks:

Facebook: King Kevin Dorival
YouTube: Kevin Dorival
Linkedin: Kevin "King" Dorival
Twitter: @Courage2Believe
Instagram: @Courage2Believe
Goodreads: Courage2Believe

**For more information on King Kevin Dorival's,
programs, products and services, contact:
www.kevindorival.com
or
Business Phone: 470-377-1126**

Hope you were blessed by reading this book. Please, share your book review on Amazon.com, Facebook, BN.com, iTunes Books, Goodreads. com, and wherever books are sold. I'll be honored to speak at your school, church, bookstore, or library's event.

For Inquires/ Life Skills and Empowerment Workshops: info@kevin-dorival.com.

Most Requested Workshop Topics:

Motivation/Keynote
African History/Haitian Revolution
Overcoming Adversity
Youth Enrichment
Leadership/Marketing

Workshop: Finding The Winner In The Mirror—Available Now

Products:

- Inspirational Autobiography: *The Courage to Believe*—Available on iTunes, Amazon, Paperback, and eBooks.
- *"7 Types of Queens, Kings Desire"*—Available Now
- Stage Play:" *The Courage to Believe"*—Available Now
- *"7 Types of Kings, Queens Desire—2023"*
- Art, Statues, and Book Collection: Divinebooksandarts.com
- Documentary: *The Courage to Believe: Never Give Up*—November 2021
- Children's book: *Prince Peter and the Magical Sparkling Book.* November 2021

Please, order <u>my book only from my website</u> since Amazon **takes 70% of the profits—I get 100% on www.kevindorival.com.

SAVING OUR YOUTH WITH YOUR SUPPORT

Courage To Believe International, Inc. is a 501(c)3 nonprofit youth mentoring organization founded in 2014 by the author. Notable programs: C2B Chess Club & Youth Mentoring Program, Annual Black-on-Black Crime Solutions Panel Movement. To donate, please visit the website: www.thecouragetobelieve.com or GoFundMe.

We are currently raising $1,000,000.00 to purchase, run, and operate the Rosette Pierre's Creative Art Center in Atlanta, Georgia, and Cap-Haïtien, Haiti. Our goal is to circumvent the school-to-prison pipeline amongst urban youth and supplying children of Haiti with education, food, and school supplies.

Trip to NASA w/C2B Chess Club & Mentoring Program, 2016

Want to support? All donations are tax-deductible—Mail Checks to:

Courage To Believe Int'l
P.O. Box 150071 Atlanta, GA. 30315

Questions/Sponsorship. We'd love to hear from you: **info@kevindorival.com**

WORKS CITED

1   Dorival, King Kevin. "Courage To Believe: Never Give Up, Keep Moving Forward," December 12, 2015. SkyView Creative Circle.

2   Dr. Maxwell Maltz. "The Magic Power of Self-Image Psychology" Prentice-Hall, November, 1964.

3   Sweeney, Michael S., "Brain The Complete Mind: How It Develops, How It Works, And How To Keep It Sharp." National Geographic, November 17, 2009

4   Dr. Ivan Van Sertima, Black Women of Antiquity. (Rochester: Transaction Publishes, 1998), 34.

5   Dr. Wilson, Amos. Black-On-Black Violence: The Psychodynamics of Black Self-Annihilation in Service of White Domination. New York City, Afrikan World InfoSystems. First Edition. 1990

6   Lieberman, Charlotte. Why You Procrastinate (It Has Nothing to Do With Self-Control). 2019. The New York Times. https://www.ny-times.com/2019/03/25/smarter-living/why-you-procrastinate-it-has-nothing-to-do-with-self-control.html

7   Byrne, Rhonda, The Secret. (Simon & Schuster; 57714th edition (January 1, 1994), 53

8   Dorival, Kevin, "7 Types of Queens, Kings Desires." Skyview Creative Circle: 2017, page 309

9   Rollin, McCraty, Ph. D., "The Science of Heart Math: The Heart-Brain Connection," https://www.heartmath.com/science/

10 McLeod, Saul. "Cognitive Dissonance," 2018, February 5. https://www.simplypsychology.org/cognitive-dissonance.html.

11 Alshami, Ali M. "Pain: Is It All in the Brain or the Heart?" November 4, 2019. Pub Med.Gov

12 James, CLR. "The Black Jacobins: Toussaint L'Ouverture and the San Domingo Revolution." (New York, Random House) 1989.

13 Clark, George P. *Phylon*, The Role of the Haitian Volunteers at Savannah in 1779: An Attempt at an Objective View. Vol. 41, No. 4 (4th Qtr., 1980), pp. 356-366

14 Aristide, Jean-Bertrand, "Toussaint L'Ouverture - François-Dominique Toussaint L'Ouverture: The Haitian Revolution" (Verso Books: 17 Oct 2008)

15 Dr. Huggins, Nathan Irvin. "Black Odyssey: The Afro-American Ordeal in Slavery" First Edition 1977. NY: Pantheon Books, 1977.

16 Clarke, John Henrik. Christopher Columbus and the Afrikan Holocaust: Slavery and the Rise of European Capitalism. A & B Books, Brooklyn, New York . New York. 1992

17 Dorival, Kevin, "Real Superhero's: Haiti's Chassuier Volunteer De Saint Dominique At The Battle Of Savannah Part 1," November 30, 2019. https://Kevindorival.Com/Real-Super-Heros-Haitis-Chassuier-Voluntter-De-Saint-Dominique-At-The-Battle-Of-Savannah-Part-1/

18 Pastor Bryant, Jamal. "I Feel Like I'm Losing It." YouTube video, 5:55. posted 2020. June 1 https://youtu.be/ zsChk9dpY0

19 Herculano-Houzel, Dr. Suzana, "The human brain in numbers: a linearly scaled-up primate brain," 2009, November 9. Frontiers in Human Neuroscience. https://www.frontiersin.org/articles/10.3389/neuro.09.031.2009/full#B28

20 Mitchum, Rob, "Neuroscientists leads unprecedented research to map billions of brain cells,"2018, May 31. The University of Chicago

21 Mitchum, Rob, "A journey to map the mind," June 25, 2018. University of Chicago https://www.uchicago.edu/features/a journey to map the mind/

22 Eliot Brown, "Guest of Honor: Booker T. Washington, Theodore Roosevelt, and the White House Dinner That Shocked a Nation" by Deborah Davis," Today I Found Out, July 17, 2012, https://www.washingtonpost.com/opinions/guest-of-honor-booker-t-washington-theodore-roosevelt-and-the-white-house-dinner-that-shocked-a-nation-by-deborah-davis/2012/08/17/f27db832-db09-11e1-bd1f-8f2b57de6d94 story.html

23 Diop, Dr. Cheikh Anta, "The African Origin of Civilization Myth or Reality." (1974 - Lawrence Hill Books.), 86.

24 Richmond, Cynthia, "Dream Power," 22. Simon & Schuster, New York, NY.

25 Towne, Rachael. "What is Kirlian Photography? Aura Photography Revealed." Updated, January 22, 2020. https://www.lightstalking.com/what-is-kirlian-photography-the-science-and-the-myth-revealed/

26 "Your Brain on H2O." University of California, Davis. 2, December 2015, https://shcs.ucdavis.edu/blog/archive/healthy-habits/your-brain-h2o

27 Goldberg, Sam, "Infrared Countermeasures: The Systems That Cool The Threat From Heat-Seeking Missiles," Air & Space Magazine, July 2003. https://www.airspacemag.com/how-things-work/infrared-countermeasures-4739633/

28 Gerloff, Pamela. "You're Not Laughing Enough, and That's No Joke. Psychology Today." Jun 21, 2011, https://www.psychologytoday.com/us/

blog/the-possibility-paradigm/201106/youre-not-laughing-enough-an
d-thats-no-joke

29 Dr. Napier, K. Nancy, "The Myth of Multitasking." May 12, 2014, https://
www.psychologytoday.com/us/blog/creativity-without-borders/201405/
the-myth-multitasking

30 Dr. Llaila Afrika. "African Holistic Health." New York City. 2004, 5th
Edition, A&B Publishers Group. (Rest In Power)

31 Sessums, Zoë, "7 Simple Ways to Use Feng Shui in Your Home." March
14, 2020. https://www.architecturaldigest.com/story/simple-ways-to-use-fen
g-shui-in-your-home

32 Anjie Cho, Anjie. "The Basic Principles of Feng Shui." May 14, 2020. https://
www.thespruce.com/what-is-feng-shui-1275060

33 World Athletics. "Olympic Games Records." https://www.worldathletics.
org/records/by-category/olympic-games-records

34 Dr. Rubik, Beverly, "Measurements of the Human Biofield and Other
Energic Instruments." https://www.faim.org/measurement-of-the-huma
n-biofield-and-other-energetic-instruments

35 Garvey, Marcus. "Marcus Garvey Life and Lessons: A Centennial
Companion to the Marcus Garvey and Universal Negro Improvement,"
University of California Press 1987.

36 Wagner, Betsy. "How Master P Turned $10,000 Into A $250 Million
Fortune," July 19, 2019. https://ca.finance.yahoo.com/news/how-master-
p-turned-10000-into-a-250-million-fortune-201641409.html

37 Yousuf, A. & Raza, S., A critical analysis of chromotherapy and its scientific
evolution. Evidence-Based Complementary and Alternative Medicine. (2005).
2(4), 481-488. http://www.trconnections.com/Colorology_Brochure.pdf

38 Gaston, A.G. "Green Power: The Successful Way of A.G. Gaston." Big City
Brands, LLC., 2013

39 Yousuf, A. & Raza, S., A critical analysis of chromotherapy and its scientific
evolution. Evidence-Based Complementary and Alternative Medicine. (2005).
2(4), 481-488. http://www.trconnections.com/Colorology_Brochure.pdf

40 "The Link Between Color and Reading Comprehension." K5 Chalkbox
https://www.k5chalkbox.com/color-and-reading-comprehension.html

41 White, C. Martha, "Locked-in Profits: The U.S. Prison Industry,
By The Numbers." NBC News. November 15, 2015. https://www.
nbcnews.com/business/business-news/locked-in-profits-u-s-priso
n-industry-numbers-n455976

42 Staff, Mayo Clinic. "Positive thinking: Stop negative self-talk to reduce stress." January 21, 2020. https://www.mayoclinic.org/healthy-lifestyle/stress-management/in-depth/positive-thinking/art-20043950

43 King, Thad. "Allyson Felix: American Athlete" 2016, November 7. https://www.britannica.com/biography/allyson-felix

44 Hart, Ryan, "What Percentage of Lottery Winners Go Broke? (Plus 35 More Statistics)" December 3, 2018. https://www.ryanhart.org/lottery-winner-statistics/

45 Theodore, "Skinner's Box Experiment," Practical Psychology: https://practicalpie.com/skinners-box-experiment/

46 African American Registry, "England's Black Queen, Sophie Charlotte born." https://aaregistry.org/story/englands-first-black-queen-sophie-charlotte-born/

47 Thomas Sankara: The Upright Man. California Newsreel. http://newsreel.org/video/thomas-sankara-the-upright-man